Tools for Tomorrow

A practical guide to strategic planning
for voluntary organisations

Professor Ian Bruce
Caroline Copeman
Andrew Forrest
Ruth Lesirge
Paul Palmer
Atul Patel

Published by NCVO
Society Building
8 All Saints Street
London N1 9RL

First published 2004.

This edition published
November 2012.

© NCVO 2012
Registered Charity Number: 225922

Design by Steers McGillanEves Ltd
Printed by The Charlesworth Press

British Library Cataloguing in
Publication Data
A catalogue record for this book is
available from the British Library

ISBN 978-0-7199-0008-2

Acknowledgements

The production of this toolkit grew out of a collaboration between the Cass Centre for Charity Effectiveness (Cass CCE) and the National Council for Voluntary Organisations (NCVO)'s Third Sector Foresight. Linda Mitchell, previously head of partnerships, and Karl Wilding, head of policy, research and foresight at NCVO, had a vision of providing practical tools to help the large number of voluntary organisations that struggle with planning, constrained as they are by firefighting, meeting income targets and controlling expenditure. Many others from NCVO have also provided invaluable input, support, comment and advice for the three editions; these include: Megan Griffith-Gray, Natalie Williams, Mike Wright, Katie Hall, Caroline Bennett, Véronique Jochum, Sarah Coombes, Kathryn Cook, Nick Wilkie, Emma King, Rebecca Forrester, Jayne Blackborow, Kim Turner, Maurice McLeod and Greg Lamyman.

Finally, it would not have been possible to produce the original toolkit without the financial support provided by the Vodafone UK Foundation, Cass CCE and the Calouste Gulbenkian Foundation.

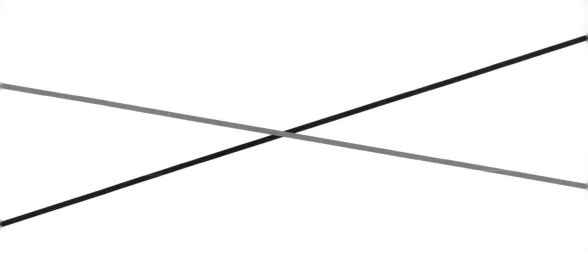

Contents

Foreword   4
The authors   6

Introduction

The purpose of the toolkit   7
How to use the toolkit   8
What is included in each tool?   10
When to use the toolkit   11
Who should get involved?   12

Stage 1 – Getting the direction right

Introduction   14
Stakeholder analysis   15
Engaging service users   16
Mission, vision and values   17
Value proposition   18

Stage 2 – Environmental analysis

Introduction   20
SWOT   21
Internal health check   22
PEST   24
Portfolio analysis   25
Dual bottom line analysis   26
Other player analysis   28
Strategic group mapping   29
Risk analysis   31
Ansoff matrix   33

Stage 3 – Options and choice

Introduction   36
Strategic options   37
Other player options   38
Force-field analysis   39
Cost-benefit analysis   41
Break-even analysis   43
Strategy screen   46

Stage 4 – Planning

Introduction   48
Goal and target setting   49
Writing a strategic plan   50
Budgeting   51

Stage 5 – Implementation

Introduction   54
Change management   55
Performance management   56
Project management   57

Stage 6 – Evaluation

Introduction   60
Assessment and reporting   61
Outcome assessment   62

Resources

Communication
and involvement tools   66
Books and web resources   70
Further support   76

Foreword
Denise Fellows

Charities increasingly recognise the need to be able to clearly communicate their vision and plans for the future to funders, beneficiaries and opinion formers. Strategic planning is a creative process, which, when done well, helps to engage, provide direction and explain the roadmap to get to a sustainable future.

Among the myriad of dry textbook approaches to developing strategic thinking, *Tools for Tomorrow* has always shone as a beacon of practicality. The demand for *Tools for Tomorrow* since it first appeared in 2004 has been high and we are delighted that a third edition is being published. We have kept the easily accessible ways of engaging with the useful tools and disciplines, which are presented alongside practical examples and explained using language with which the sector is familiar. The authors are all academics who have worked extensively within the voluntary, community and social enterprise sector.

Many thanks once again to Caroline Copeman, who led the project, and to NCVO for this fruitful collaboration.

Please remember that Cass CCE provides regular events that bring you up-to-date thinking about developing strategy throughout the year and you can join our network by emailing casscce@city.ac.uk. Contact details and more information about our programmes and services can be found at the back of the toolkit.

Wishing you successful planning!

Denise Fellows
Director and CEO
Cass CCE Consultancy
and Talent Development

Foreword
Karl Wilding

Supporting trustees and managers to build strong, impactful voluntary organisations is at the heart of NCVO's mission. We have long recognised that effective strategic planning is fundamental to the long-term health and impact of voluntary organisations, so I am delighted to write the introduction to this new edition of *Tools for Tomorrow*.

Tools for Tomorrow is the practical partner to NCVO's Third Sector Foresight programme, which aims to provide organisations with actionable intelligence about the environment within which they operate. Foresight – and this guide – was originally conceived in response to the concern that organisations spent too much time fire fighting and not enough time on strategy; that equal focus should be given to the forces outside the organisation shaping it; and that tools were needed to help organisations make sense of complex, seemingly voluminous information.

So, this new edition of *Tools for Tomorrow* aims to help you separate the signal from the noise. It aims to support you in charting the roadmap to your organisation's future. And it is based upon the reasoning that although harsh economic and social forces buffet our organisations, we can shape our own futures.

Finally, I'm delighted that Caroline Copeman, who was integral to the original ideas and plans that made *Tools for Tomorrow* one of NCVO's best-selling publications, has worked with us on this edition. Caroline has completely revised and updated the text so that *Tools for Tomorrow* is at the forefront of strategy and planning.

I hope you enjoy reading – and using – this publication as much as I have.

Karl Wilding
Head of Policy and Research
NCVO

The authors

The authors all work at Cass CCE.

Ian Bruce is the president of Cass CCE and his particular interest is strategic planning and marketing for charities. He is vice-president of the Royal National Institute of Blind People and was previously chief executive of two national charities, a chief officer in local government and manager in the private sector.

Caroline Copeman edited the toolkit and is a senior visiting fellow and principal consultant at Cass CCE. She has 20 years' senior experience in the commercial, public and voluntary sectors and has a particular interest in strategy development and business planning, human resource management, change management, governance, leadership and organisational development.

Andrew Forrest is a tutor on the Cass CCE degree programme, a principal consultant at Cass CCE, and was director of learning and development at The Work Foundation. He specialises in the development and training of senior managers in all sectors and in helping organisations through mentoring, coaching and secondments.

Ruth Lesirge is a recognised figure in adult and community education, particularly with adults returning to study and management development, and is a tutor on Cass CCE's degree programme. She has a special interest in chief executive, board and trustee development.

Paul Palmer is professor of voluntary sector management and an associate dean at the Cass Business School responsible for Ethics, Sustainability and Engagement. He is also the director of the CCE, incorporating research, consultancy and five master's degree courses focusing on the voluntary sector.

Atul Patel is leader of the Cass CCE MSc in voluntary sector management, is qualified in social work and has spent more than 15 years working in the voluntary and statutory sectors. His particular interests are in management development, strategy development, diversity management, assessment of complex staffing situations and advising trustees.

Introduction

The purpose of the toolkit

The purpose of this toolkit is to produce a straightforward guide that will help trustees and managers to find a suitable pathway through the stages of strategic planning. All organisations, no matter what size they are, face the challenge of asking questions about their position, making choices based on the answers and developing action plans for change: this is what strategic planning is all about – stimulating strategic thinking and acting. Planning can be simple and straightforward, particularly if it is made more accessible and relevant. Above all, it is a creative process that brings demonstrable benefits: there is a direct link between effective planning and long-term sustainability, and it is the first step towards sustainable funding.

The toolkit has been designed to be used by every type of voluntary and community organisation, and by those who work with them as consultants or advisers. We considered developing different tools according to the nature of work or size of organisation, but quickly realised that these tools could be applied across all. We have picked out the 27 most helpful tools or areas of good practice and written some simple guidelines about how to use them. The toolkit is structured so that users can take a 'pick and mix' approach – selecting only the tools they need or have the resources to apply.

Our principles in developing the toolkit were:

- each tool can stand alone, so that you can decide what resources you have available, and select the tools to meet your organisation's needs; we give guidance about what tools we think are vital. While we recommend that the tools are followed as we suggest (at least at first), they are suitable for adaptation to meet your organisation's needs

- if we found that we could not fit the description of how to use the tool on one or two sides of A4, we abandoned it; the idea was to keep the process as simple as possible

- the toolkit will signpost you to other resources that can be used to supplement the kit in case you get bitten by the planning bug (or find it all too complicated and want a training course or a bit of consultancy help)

- the guide doesn't attempt to be an academic reference book; there are plenty of those around already

- strategy work is decidedly not just a top-down process, so all the tools are designed for use by groups from across your organisation; tips on communication and involvement, plus a tool on getting service users involved, are also included

- we believe that what happens in management is a mix of what is intended (planned for) and what emerges unexpectedly; the planning process we follow encourages the inclusion of ideas that emerge from everyday activity.

The toolkit is designed to be used by trustees, management teams and staff. We believe that everyone, led by the board or management committee, has a role to play in strategic planning and there is a section about who should get involved.

We want to encourage organisations to carry out planning throughout the year (and avoid it being a rushed job just before the budget or a submission to a funder is due). You need to be nimble and ready to respond to new challenges and opportunities as they emerge. However, it is inevitable that the process will have an annual cycle, with particularly intensive activity in the three months or so prior to the start of the financial year. We have included a section to help make judgements about when to start things; some activities repeat on an annual basis, others need only be done every two or three years.

How to use the toolkit

We have divided the strategic planning process up into six stages; each stage has a number of 'tools' or 'good practice guides' associated with it. Where there is an established technique for developing strategy or planning we've incorporated this into a tool; where we have come across good practice in a particular area, we have captured this in a good practice guide.

Listed below is a description of each of the stages, with the tools we have included for each.

Stage	Tool/Good practice guide
1. Getting the direction right We see the strategic planning process as a journey with a number of stages. There are some opportunities for short cuts and some vital steps that must be taken. Being sure about where you are going, your desired future and whether this is the right future for the organisation, comprise the important first stage. Starting with the board, all those involved with the organisation have a contribution to make.	• Stakeholder analysis • Engaging service users • Mission, vision and values • Value proposition
2. Environmental analysis Early on, it is important to assess the challenges and opportunities that the organisation is likely to face, as well as how fit the organisation is to carry out its work. This assessment of what is happening (now and in the foreseeable future) both internally and externally will form a backdrop for future decision making.	• SWOT • Internal health check • PEST • Portfolio analysis • Dual bottom line analysis • Other player analysis • Strategic group mapping • Risk analysis • Ansoff matrix
3. Options and choice It is likely that there are a number of options for how to achieve the desired future. These options need to be explored so that an informed decision can be made about what actions are needed. This isn't just about choice, but also priority, feasibility and risk assessment.	• Strategic options • Other player options • Force-field analysis • Cost-benefit analysis • Break-even analysis • Strategy screen

When you come to look at each of the individual tools and good practice guides, you will see that we have used icons to differentiate between tools that are vital for effective strategic planning and those that can be useful, depending on the circumstances. In the next section, we show how we've tried to help you make decisions about which tools to choose.

 Vital   Useful

Stage	Tool/Good practice guide
4. Planning At a suitable point in the journey trustees and staff need to take stock, review all the information generated, sort it and get down to the basics of planning the next steps in detail. Often at this stage organisations like to document the actions in a written plan. Documenting the actions doesn't mean that they are carved in stone – new strategies and actions will always need to be encouraged.	• Goal and target setting • Writing a strategic plan • Budgeting
5. Implementation Once decisions have been made about the future direction and the actions needed to achieve this desired future, the management actions (often expressed as goals, targets and outcomes) need to be built into everyday life – embedded in the systems and processes of the organisation. Often these actions are a mix of continuing to do the things that have always been done (but maybe do them better), plus new projects to implement new initiatives.	• Change management • Performance management • Project management
6. Evaluation Progress needs to be assessed at appropriate reporting intervals to make sure things are on track, heading in the right direction and continuing to achieve the outcomes established at the start (delivering the desired impact). It is really motivating to have achievements discussed and reported, not just for members of the organisation, but also for service users and funders.	• Assessment and reporting • Outcome management

What is included in each tool?

Our approach with each of the tools and good practice guides is to provide you with:

- a description of what the tool or good practice guide is about
- the benefits and limitations of using the tool or good practice guide
- when to use it
- how to use it
- in some cases, an illustration to help explain the detail.

When to use the toolkit

1. Getting the direction right – periodic

- Revisit the vision and values every 8 to 10 years.
- Review the mission about every three to five years.
- Neither of these activities need to be within the planning cycle (you can take it at a more leisurely pace).

2. Environmental analysis – periodic, ongoing and annual

- You can make PEST and other player analysis an ongoing activity. Find a simple way of collecting and updating external data as people pick up on changes.
- Start the other elements at least three months before plans are due.
- Think about a detailed review every three years, with smaller scale annual planning activities in between.

3. Options and choices – annual

- All too often this stage is rushed, when it should have the biggest time investment.
- Start at least three months in advance of plans being due (this may depend on the frequency of board meetings).
- Expect big changes every three years and build more time in then.

4. Planning – annual

- Once the thinking is done, capture it and start to cascade it across the organisation (and to external stakeholders).
- Your timescale here might be dictated for you.
- You may choose to do a high level strategic plan around every three years, with a detailed annual business plan that just needs to be updated each year.

5. Implementation – ongoing

- Once you've established the frameworks, plans and programmes should just be updated and roll on seamlessly.
- New projects will need to be incorporated.

6. Evaluation – ongoing

- Again, once the new targets and outcomes have been updated, things should roll on seamlessly.

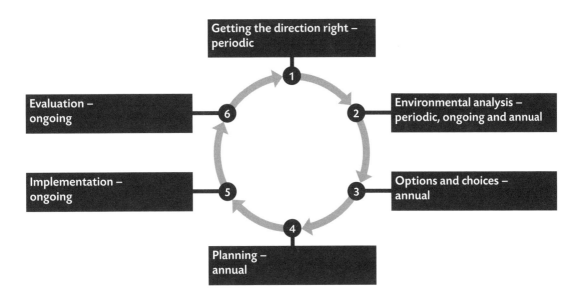

Introduction

Who should get involved?

Strategic planning affects the whole organisation, so it is imperative that everyone feels part of the development process. Ultimate responsibility and decision making is the role of the board, supported by the chief executive, management team and staff. External stakeholders, such as service users and other beneficiaries, have an important part to play, as do others, such as funders, policy makers and potential partners.

Links between strategy and governance: a trustee board perspective

- Trustees are legally accountable for the direction and work of the organisation.
- Trustees are at arm's length to the work so they can have a useful overview.
- Trustees hold the long-term health of the organisation in trust for future beneficiaries; they can put an alternative case to the shorter-term imperatives that may preoccupy staff.
- They may have experience of the longer-term history and issues of the organisation that may impact on planning.
- They can contribute moods or views 'from the outside' when assessing the PR or public support considerations.

For all those who get involved, there are some things to think about

- Strategic planning needs the best information, experience and expertise that the partnership of staff, chief executive and trustees can provide together.
- There is never only one right answer.
- There is no perfect strategy – every solution generates new challenges.
- The trust and goodwill of trustees and staff is crucial – it builds corporate commitment to the planning.
- The strategic conversation that goes on across the organisation is as important as the plan – it mobilises and gives ownership and involvement.

The key players are:

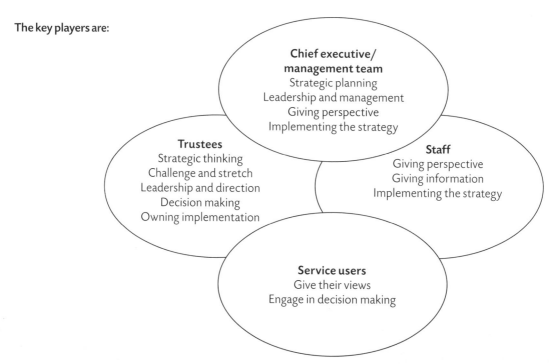

Chief executive/
management team
Strategic planning
Leadership and management
Giving perspective
Implementing the strategy

Trustees
Strategic thinking
Challenge and stretch
Leadership and direction
Decision making
Owning implementation

Staff
Giving perspective
Giving information
Implementing the strategy

Service users
Give their views
Engage in decision making

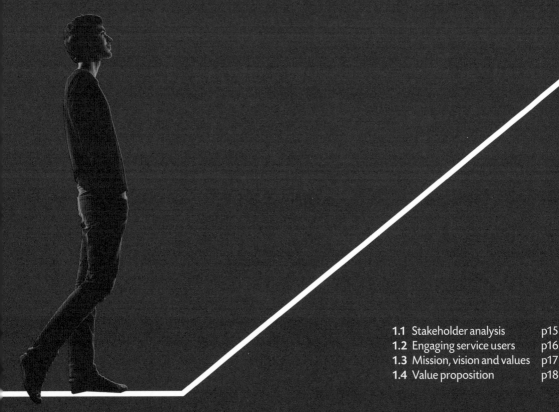

Stage 1
Getting the direction right

1.1 Stakeholder analysis   p15
1.2 Engaging service users   p16
1.3 Mission, vision and values   p17
1.4 Value proposition   p18

Getting the direction right

Strategic planning is a key driver for sustained organisational effectiveness. The first step in the process is to make sure that the direction in which the organisation is moving is the right one and that it meets the needs of stakeholders, including service users and clients, who are at the heart of every voluntary and community organisation.

Organisations usually have some kind of broad statement (or series of statements) that capture the strategic direction. We use the three most common definitions: mission, vision and values, and include a tool to help you define or review these statements.

We suggest that you look in detail at the overall direction of the organisation (and consult stakeholders as a major strategic exercise) once every three to five years. This should be sufficient to make sure that your purpose remains relevant and you have a strategic direction that stretches and challenges you as well as keeps pace with the changes you face.

How you deliver your mission in detail will need to be reviewed more frequently (with the mission as the backdrop). We call the statements that capture how you deliver your mission, 'strategic objectives' and 'annual goals'. Some organisations choose to carry out a big strategic review about every three years and develop long-term strategic objectives that they intend to last for about three years. Thinking in terms of a hierarchy of direction, the whole thing may look like this:

Vision and values
Review every 8 to 10 years.

Mission
Review every three to five years.

Strategic objectives
Set as part of a major strategic planning exercise, strategic objectives will deliver the mission for the next three years and should be developed to be relevant for about three years.

Annual goals
Set each year as part of a smaller-scale annual planning exercise, these annual goals will deliver the strategic objectives and should be relevant for about the next 12 months.

Tools included in this section
Stakeholder analysis   p15
Engaging service users   p16
Mission, vision and values   p17
Value proposition   p18

1.1 Stakeholder analysis Tool

What is it?

Stakeholder analysis is the identification of your organisation's key stakeholders, an assessment of their interests and the ways in which these interests impact on your organisation.

A stakeholder is a person, group or organisation that has an interest in your organisation. Stakeholders:

- have needs and expectations
- can be internal or external to your organisation
- can be further divided into direct and intermediary stakeholders.

Direct stakeholders are connected to your organisation, for example, funders, the Charity Commission and your service users. Intermediary stakeholders are not directly connected but may still have an interest in you, for example, MPs.

Why should you use it?

Benefits It enables you to establish good relations with your stakeholders by developing stakeholder strategies that relate directly to how important the stakeholder is to you.

Limitations Everyone in an organisation has a different perception of who the stakeholders are and what importance they may have. Lack of agreement on this may cause conflict and tensions.

When should you use it?

⭐ **Vital** about every two years, and whenever you review your mission, vision and values.

It's vital to engage your service users in this process; be very clear about their needs and expectations, and make sure their level of influence and interest in you are appropriate to your mission.

How to use the tool

- Draw up a 'stakeholder table' for all stakeholders (see table below).
- Do an assessment of each stakeholder's interest in your organisation and their influence (or power) over you.
- Map them on the interest/ influence matrix (see diagram below) and decide on strategies for each stakeholder group according to where they are on the matrix, where you'd like them to be and what it will take to shift them.
- Use a team approach to wordstorm the issues, making sure you involve staff and trustees.

Consider interviewing or sending questionnaires to key external stakeholders; see the special tool about engaging service users.

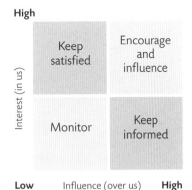

Name of stakeholder	Degree of interest in us (H,M,L)	Degree of influence over us (H,M,L)	Stakeholder expectations and needs	Attitudes to our performance

1.2 Engaging service users
Good practice guide

What is it?

This good practice guide helps to structure your thinking on how to engage service users (beneficiaries, clients, members, consumers, customers) in strategic planning.

Why should you use it?

Benefits It provides a framework to start the process of user involvement (UI) and helps to clarify your thinking and planning around this.

Limitations This guide can only offer a framework – you will need to think about what will work in your organisation.

When should you use it?

★ **Vital** at all stages of the strategic planning process, not just at the start. UI can be particularly helpful when reviewing the mission and vision of the organisation.

How to use the guide

Whatever your motivation for developing UI, there are some key steps to take to kick-start it and a range of different ways of engaging users. It is important to recognise that while there are some general principles to follow, there is no single 'off the peg' formula for successful UI – much depends on the nature of your client group, the size of your organisation and the type of issues facing your organisation.

Key steps[1]

1. Ask yourself 'How could involving users contribute to improved organisational effectiveness and sustainability?'

2. Develop some desired outcomes so you can shape the process and measure the impact of the UI measures you adopt.

3. Think through where you most want input – be realistic and honest about how much influence people can have.

4. Gain support and participation for the UI initiative from senior people in the organisation – make sure UI isn't in a 'vacuum'.

5. Put yourself in the users' shoes or ask what techniques and approaches might help them to offer the kind of feedback you are looking for – make the UI events fun and participative.

6. Give feedback to users and champion the outcomes of UI internally – demonstrate how UI makes a difference.

7. Overall, treat UI participants extremely well – as you would a new funder or a group of trustees.

Different ways of engaging users[2]

Give information	Ask for feedback	Involve in creating things	Involve in decisions
Produce newsletters on paper or online	User page in the newsletter or discussion group on website	User council, conference or 'Parliament'	Recruit users to the board
Produce important information in accessible, easy language	Suggestion box	'Meet the CEO' type sessions	Involve users in staff recruitment and induction
	User survey or questionnaire	Focus groups	Involve in working parties
	UI teams – dedicated staff	Users carry out staff awareness training	
		Self-help groups	

[1] With thanks to Speaking Up!
[2] With thanks to United Response

1.3 Mission, vision and values Tool

What is it?

Mission, vision and values are the three key components that form the purpose of an organisation. Together they make up the very basis of what an organisation is about. The vision is a compelling description of the future; it is about how you want the future to be. The mission describes the business of your organisation; it conveys what your organisation is there to do, and therefore how it contributes to achieving the vision. The value statement describes the way you work, your behaviour and the enduring traits, beliefs, convictions and characteristics that are deemed to be important and worthwhile to your organisation.

Why should you use it?

Benefits Developing your vision, mission and value statement can:
- give your organisation a long-term view
- unite the organisation around a common sense of purpose and identity
- communicate clearly to your internal/external stakeholders what your organisation is about
- create a sense of purpose from which a strategy can be developed.

Limitations There is no agreed terminology when it comes to these headings; they can mean different things to different people and can cause tension and conflict when discussing them.

When should you use it?

⭐ **Vital** if your organisation doesn't have a statement of its mission, vision and values, you should seriously consider developing one. If you already have one in place, you should re-look at the vision and values every 8 to 10 years and review the continuing relevance of your mission about every three to five years.

How to use the tool

When developing or reviewing your mission, vision and values, check for the following features in each one of them. Everyone in the organisation needs to be involved, led by the trustees. See page 66 for tips on setting up focus groups and away days.

A good vision:
- describes the future you want
- is about the heart and the head, and is idealistic in tone
- conveys a standard of excellence
- reflects horizon-expanding ideals
- inspires enthusiasm and commitment
- is easily understood and accessible to all
- is congruent with the mission
- involves bringing about change.

Your mission statement should say:
- who you are
- what you do
- why you do it
- how you do it
- why you exist.

It should be:
- clear and easily understood
- short and focused
- inspiring (internally and externally)
- realistic, workable and achievable
- expressed in terms of outcomes
- congruent with charitable objectives (if it isn't, then these should be reviewed too).

Features of values:
- people feel they have value or worth, and hold them dear
- they are beliefs, attitudes or principles expressed in behaviours
- they govern organisational behaviour – what people do and how they do it, for example, valuing diversity and equal opportunities
- they should be consistent with each other and with vision and mission.

Getting the direction right

1.4 Value proposition Tool

What is it?

A value proposition is the difference you make, and the value you add to your stakeholders' experiences. Stakeholders may be members, service users, policy makers, commissioners, donors and so on. This value is expressed in terms of their experience, rather than what you do or say. So, it's a reduction in debt, not an easy-access debt helpline; it's a fulfilling family life, not a flat in sheltered housing.

An understanding of the value you create for your stakeholders, expressed in terms of the experience they seek, enables you to really test out the extent to which your organisation is oriented towards delivering this value. If activities aren't wholly oriented towards delivering value, you should really question why you're doing them.

Why should you use it?

Benefits It stimulates a focus on the things that are important (and helps you get rid of the things that aren't). Your relationship with donors, commissioners and policy makers, as well as relationships with service users and members, will benefit from this greater consideration, especially when you involve them in the conversation.

Limitations It can be quite a complex and multidimensional analysis, and

often a range of views emerge that can be very different but equally valid. You need to be open to working with a range of perceptions and opinions as you consider what they mean for your strategy.

When should you use it?

⬤ **Useful** to supplement stakeholder analysis when you want to engage trustees and senior external stakeholders (such as commissioners or funders) in refreshing your strategy: you'll all be looking at strategy through a different lens from normal.

How to use the tool

- List the range of stakeholders your organisation engages with.
- Ponder their needs and wants: what lies at the root of their interaction with you? Why do they do it? What do they want?
- Consider the value experience they seek from you as you deliver your services, campaigns or products. Write this down as it is at the heart of the discussion you need to have with trustees and other senior stakeholders as you explore how you really add value to stakeholders' experiences.
- Complete the table below. The final column is about evidence – you need to have evidence of the true value you add so you can be sure

that your strategy is working.
- You may then want to consider other organisations that also deliver value to your stakeholders. How do they meet the experience needs of these stakeholders? Who does it best? What can you learn? What must you stop doing or start doing differently?

Once you are clear about your range of value propositions, you can then think about the processes that deliver them by considering the following questions.

- To what extent is everything you do focused on delivering and achieving these specific results? What activities are not focused on delivering the value experience? Should you be doing them? How might you do them differently and change the impact they have?
- How can the activities that contribute to the value experience be improved to deliver an even better experience?
- How can you add to the experience or to the cost effectiveness of delivering the experience?
- Are there patterns across the value experience needs of different stakeholder groups? Where is there consistency? Are there any clashes? How will this affect your strategy?

Make sure you also think about where you work with others to deliver the value experience, as well as when you work on your own.

Stakeholder group (think about different groups – service users, funders, policy makers etc)	Value experience sought (as perceived by each stakeholder group)	Products, campaigns or services offered to deliver this value experience	How the offering delivers clear value	How the value delivered differentiates your organisation	The evidence you have of the difference made

Stage 2
Environmental analysis

2.1 SWOT   p21
2.2 Internal health check   p22
2.3 PEST   p24
2.4 Portfolio analysis   p25
2.5 Dual bottom line analysis   p26
2.6 Other player analysis   p28
2.7 Strategic group mapping   p29
2.8 Risk analysis   p31
2.9 Ansoff matrix   p33

Environmental analysis

Early on in the strategic planning process, it is important to assess the challenges and opportunities that the organisation is likely to face, as well as how fit the organisation is to carry out its mission.

This assessment of what is happening (now and in the foreseeable future) will form a backdrop for future decision making and is called environmental analysis. Environmental analysis looks at both internal and external issues, and takes in both the current state and the likely future.

Most tools in this section look at specifics – what's going on outside the organisation (PEST), the internal state of health (internal health check), what other players in your marketplace are doing (other player analysis and strategic group mapping). Some of these tools may only be relevant about every three years. SWOT is a more general tool, and it is vital to use it each year.

Environmental analysis will give you an indication of:

- things you are already working on that need to be amended, adapted or improved
- opportunities that need to be considered for future activity
- threats that have to be considered and counter activities that should be built into plans.

You should expect to emerge from environmental analysis with a clearer picture of the challenges you face and how fit you are to meet them, plus a list of potential things to do – options or activities.

Tools included in this section

SWOT	p21
Internal health check	p22
PEST	p24
Portfolio analysis	p25
Dual bottom line analysis	p26
Other player analysis	p28
Strategic group mapping	p29
Risk analysis	p31
Ansoff matrix	p33

2.1 SWOT Tool

What is it?

An assessment of internal strengths and weaknesses, enabling an organisation to develop a strategy that will build on strengths and eliminate/minimise things that are not done so well. The tool also enables organisations to look outside themselves, at future potential opportunities and threats, and consider these when developing strategic options.

Why should you use it?

Benefits It helps to open up critical thinking across the spectrum of everything you do.

Limitations It's tempting to wordstorm a list and think you've finished. This is just the start.

When should you use it?

★ **Vital** once you are sure of the organisation's mission. Use this as the backdrop to your environmental analysis, on an annual basis.

You can expand on SWOT by doing an internal health check to get more detail on strengths and weaknesses, and PEST to get greater insights into opportunities and threats.

How to use the tool

Think through your future direction and the mission you have to achieve, and then draw the SWOT matrix:

Strengths	Weaknesses
What do we do well and have working in our favour?	In what areas is our performance not so good?

Opportunities	Threats
What trends or changes in the external environment could we take advantage of?	What trends or changes in the external environment could have a negative impact on us?

Steps

1. Go through each box, explore the positives and negatives, and come up with a list of the strategic issues facing the organisation.

2. When thinking about the internal strengths and weaknesses, consider things like:
- services, user and stakeholder satisfaction, external relationships, image
- skills/expertise, systems, trustees and staff – motivation, learning, capability, leadership
- reserves and resources including property and other capital assets, income, existing partnerships, management of costs, management of risk

- future capacity, trends and potential, as well as the current state; how sustainable is your organisation?
- what you don't do (and perhaps should).

3. When thinking about potential opportunities and threats (over, say, the next three years), consider changes to things like:
- demographics and family structures, attitudes and values
- government policy and the economy, technology and communications.

4. Refine the list by working out what's really important – the high priority issues.

5. Consider the implications – ask 'So what does this mean to us and our service users?'

6. Consider what you could do to accentuate the positive and eliminate (or minimise) the negative, ie strategies to manage the issues.

7. It's easy to focus on the negatives, so make sure you get a balance.

8. Remember that sometimes things can be both strengths and weaknesses.

2.2 Internal health check Tool

What is it?

An internal health check is an internal evaluation framework to help an organisation highlight areas for improvement and set an action agenda for strategic change.

Why should you use it?

Benefits It enables a thorough review of internal capabilities and processes.

Limitations It can produce rather a long list of things to do and can be time consuming.

When should you use it?

● **Useful** to supplement the first two elements of SWOT and to add greater depth to this analysis, perhaps every two to three years.

How to use the tool

Use the following rating framework to stimulate discussion, making sure you prioritise.

External perspective
Rate how well you:

- meet funder and service user needs
- influence policy and practice
- get external recognition
- are accountable and transparent in dealing with the community
- are accessible to outsiders
- are active in and engaged with other organisations
- access power institutions, for example, funders and local authorities.

Mission and strategy
Rate how well you:

- achieve your goals
- perform in meeting your service, business and social outcomes
- deliver the impact associated with your mission
- communicate core values and beliefs
- share a cohesive and common identity
- link high-level goals with the front-line work of the organisation.

Leadership
Rate how well you:

- link governance and executive direction
- communicate what is important
- do what you say you will (and do it how you say you will)
- perform as a team (across and up/down the organisation)
- exercise power and resolve conflict
- align people (staff and volunteers) towards achieving the mission.

Management practice
Rate how well you:

- practise effective governance
- acquire and allocate financial resource
- use all resources to build future capacity
- manage resources such as IT and premises
- understand and manage risk
- manage performance
- develop strategy
- recruit, retain and develop people
- run core services
- develop new services
- respond to new opportunities.

Learning and growth

Rate how well you:

- stimulate creativity
- motivate and inspire at all levels
- match tasks and skills, and build capacity for the future
- delegate authority, have appropriate levels of participation and use of discretion
- manage change
- manage knowledge
- involve and include people (manage diversity).

Turn your list of how well/not so well you operate into actions for improvement and put them in order of priority.

Environmental analysis

2.3 PEST Tool

What is it?

PEST is a tool to help you explore the likely future external environment (trends, opportunities, threats) under a series of headings – political, economic, social and technological. The aim is to identify the implications for your organisation.

Why should you use it?

Benefits Prompts you to think externally and into the future across the range of factors that influence organisational development.

Limitations The headings themselves can be limiting – try to think beyond them. Some use PESTEL – adding environmental and legal.

When should you use it?

Useful to supplement SWOT, perhaps every couple of years. You can carry out PEST analysis as a regular/ongoing activity by updating a set of monitoring criteria to help you keep abreast of changes.

How to use the tool

Use the headings to prompt ideas about what the different drivers for change might be in the future (try to think over the next three years); when you think of an issue, concentrate on asking, 'So what might this mean for us?' to draw out the implications.

Once you've listed the forces or trends and the implications, prioritise them (maybe around likelihood and impact), and then think about how you can maximise them (for opportunities) or minimise them (for threats).

Once again, you are developing a picture of the strategic issues facing your organisation in preparation for developing strategies to handle them.

Political	Economic
• Local as well as national • Government as funder • Legislative agenda • Infrastructure review • Public policy agenda	• Funding trends • Giving and volunteering • Economic uncertainty • Focus on outcomes and measurement

Social	Technological
• Attitudes/expectations • International conflict/insecurity • Demographic changes • Public attitudes	• Advances, pace of change, wider access • Harnessing potential • Skill requirements • Rates of obsolescence

2.4 Portfolio analysis
Tool

What is it?

A portfolio analysis helps you to look at your portfolio of products, services and campaign ideas to make decisions about where to invest more or less time and money or delete a product from the portfolio.

Why should you use it?

Benefits Many charities want to add new products/offerings before the previous ones have fulfilled their potential; this tool introduces logic to the decision making.

Limitations It was developed with an assumption that long-term profitability is the dominant goal, and responsibility to existing customers secondary – a balance of assumptions that does not sit easily in our sector. However, provided you are aware of this, it can be a very useful tool, primarily for products/offerings that break even (or have the potential to).

When should you use it?

Useful to use after SWOT and other player analysis, particularly if you feel your organisation is spreading itself too thinly.

How to use the tool

You need to place all your products/ offerings onto a matrix with two axes as in the one below.

1. The best place for your offering to be is bottom right. You have all the advantages of the highest volume provider (ie economies of scale) and although continuing investment is necessary, it will not be as high relatively as in two of the other quadrants.

   ACTION: invest significant time and money and defend at all costs.

2. The next best place to be is top right where, once again, you are market leader but the advantage is that the market is expanding rapidly so expansion is possible. This position has the disadvantage that you need to invest more heavily to make sure you get the majority of the new customers coming into the market (in order to stay market leader), so the investment cost per customer is higher than in 1 (above).

   ACTION: invest as heavily as possible.

3. Top left means you are in a rapidly growing market (and therefore have to invest heavily) but you are not market leader. You may invest a lot of money and get nowhere.

   ACTION: assess carefully to see if heavy investment can get you to the top slot. If your relative market share is low you will need some very good reasons not to exit.

4. Apparently the worst position to be in is bottom left, where you have low relative market share. Because these offerings have been around a long time, the organisation will be over loyal to them when exiting might be the best answer. If such action is not always clear in the commercial world, it is even less obvious in the charity world, where exiting may leave a cohort of vulnerable customers without help. The offering may also be popular with donors. Careful exit strategies are necessary.

   ACTION: exit or reduce costs/ raise income or donations to make them less of a drain on resources.

? or problem child (minor player in a high growth market)	**Star offering** (market leader in new high growth market)
Dog (minor player in a static market)	**Goldmine or cash cow** (market leader in a large but fairly static market)

Market growth rate ↑

Relative market share →

Environmental analysis

2.5 Dual bottom line analysis
New tool

What is it?

The dual bottom line analysis is about having:

1. a relevant and impactful portfolio of activities

2. sufficient working capital (funds to continue operations) to meet the needs and activities of the organisation over the medium to longer term.

These two elements are critically important in whether a voluntary and community organisation can continue to exist. This tool recognises the reality that many voluntary and community organisations face: income generation activities often compensate for services or campaigns that make a loss but have an impact. Having a balanced portfolio is important (although ideally all your activities will make a surplus).

This analysis helps you to explore your whole portfolio of activities to see how they exist in relation to each other. It also helps you to consider the extent to which each activity contributes to the impact you seek to have and the surplus you need to make to afford your activities and invest in a viable future for your beneficiaries.

Why should you use it?

Benefits It enables an exploration of all the organisation's activities (not just services or campaigns) to assess the extent to which each contributes to the dual bottom line (impact and surplus), and sets this up as a comparison that shows the relative merits of each.

Limitations Some activities are hard to quantify in terms of impact and surplus, but the conversation and improved understanding often make it worthwhile trying.

When should you use it?

Useful to offer a different set of insights to the portfolio analysis. The two tools can be used in alternate years to give a different perspective. Some organisations have found this tool to be very beneficial in staff workshops to illustrate why a loss-making service or campaign needs to be challenged about how it makes a difference to the lives of users (even if it's been around for years).

How to use the tool

1. List all your organisation's clusters of activities. Examples may include all the:

- services
- campaigns
- income generation approaches
- research projects
- programmes of policy development
- communications tools or initiatives.

2. Plot these activity clusters on the matrix below according to the extent to which each has impact and generates a surplus (revenue minus costs). You could draw a 'bubble' that represents each one's relative size. Bell, Masaoka and Zimmerman[1] offer an impact ranking criteria on a scale of 1–4 according to:

- fit with mission
- excellence
- scale of impact
- depth of impact
- filling an important gap (FIG)
- community building
- leverage
- financial break-even point (BEP).

3. Finally, scrutinise the whole portfolio and challenge each cluster as you develop your future strategy. The matrix below gives suggestions about tactics.

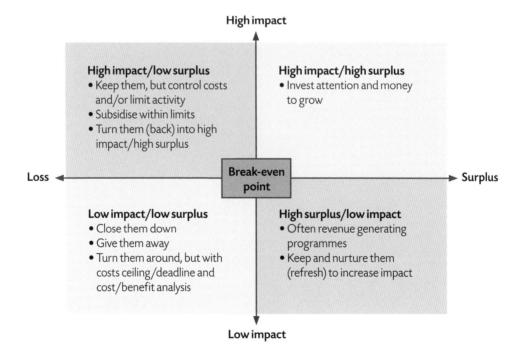

High impact

High impact/low surplus
- Keep them, but control costs and/or limit activity
- Subsidise within limits
- Turn them (back) into high impact/high surplus

High impact/high surplus
- Invest attention and money to grow

Loss ←

Break-even point

→ Surplus

Low impact/low surplus
- Close them down
- Give them away
- Turn them around, but with costs ceiling/deadline and cost/benefit analysis

High surplus/low impact
- Often revenue generating programmes
- Keep and nurture them (refresh) to increase impact

Low impact

[1] Bell J., Masaoka J. and Zimmerman S. (2010) Nonprofit Sustainability: Making strategic decisions for financial viability. San Francisco: Jossey Bass.

Environmental analysis

2.6 Other player analysis
Tool

What is it?

The other player analysis looks at the work and impact of other organisations working in the same field, in order to assess how/what they are doing, so you can make informed choices about the types of relationships you might develop with them. These could be: charities, commercial organisations, statutory organisations and, in certain situations, the 'informal sector' (friends, families and neighbours); they also may be competitors, suppliers or partners.

Why should you use it?

Benefits It helps you identify the market you are operating in, who the other players are and what they do. It also helps you determine who is potentially a partner, competitor or collaborator.

Limitations It is possible to overdo the other player analysis. You should aim to create an overview of your market.

When should you use it?

 Vital as part of your annual assessment of the external environment.

How to use the tool

Wherever possible follow the following steps.

1. Define the scope and nature of your area of activity or market[1] – reviewing your current outputs will give you a good idea of your market.

2. Determine who your beneficiaries are and what they expect.

3. Determine who the other players are.

4. Develop an individual profile of the players.

5. Determine what the key success factors[2] are in your market and how you and the other players compare – assess how well you all deliver what's important for success. Use the table below as a guide.

Questions to ask	Other player profile	Sources of information
• Who are the other players (may also include funders/donors)? • Are they competitors or partners/potential partners? • What are the other players' objectives? • What strategies are the other players pursuing and how successful are they? • What are their strengths and weaknesses? • What are the relationships like between them?	• Background • Financial information (annual reviews) • Products • Marketing strategies • Facilities • Personnel • Effectiveness	• Internet • Personal visits • Talking to service users • Advertisements • Presentations • Conference/trade show displays • Publications

[1] The market can be defined as individuals (eg service users) using your outputs, and purchasers (eg funders such as local authorities) who buy your outputs on behalf of service users. Both these groups may, for whatever reason, exercise the choice of going to other players who provide similar services. Your market may be affected by factors such as geography, the type of service user and purchaser and their needs, the activities your organisation is involved in and the other players.

[2] Key success factors in your market may be defined by the level of demand for your outputs, the sustained level of resources the players in your market attract, the reputation of players for quality of outputs, the level of interest taken by policy makers such as local/national government and the value and importance of managing equality and diversity.

2.7 Strategic group mapping Tool

What is it?

Strategic group mapping is a way of looking at your marketplace and other players through the eyes of your beneficiaries, by considering their needs.

Why should you use it?

Benefits It provides another way of looking at things, so it will help you ask different sorts of questions about your future strategy, about relations with other players and about the extent to which you meet beneficiary needs.

Limitations You may raise more questions than you can answer. And like other tools and matrices, it is very one dimensional, but it is a starting point to further thinking.

When should you use it?

Useful as part of external environment analysis and as an optional extra to other player analysis when you need more depth or a fresh way of looking at things.

How to use the tool

1. List the top five other players in your strategic group: organisations in your specialist sector or your field of operation. These would usually be organisations who provide similar services to yours, or who work with the same beneficiary group.

2. Develop a profile for each by asking the following questions:

- What services do they provide?
- What beneficiary group do they work with?
- What's their impact? What might their plans be for the future?
- How might you create greater impact by reconsidering your relationship with them?

3. It's important not only to think about who these other players are, but also about the marketplace you each work in and how this could affect your future strategies. To help with this, think about the two most important factors driving success (or ensuring outcomes) for your service users or beneficiaries. What are the most important aspects of your service (or campaign) for beneficiaries? What do they want most from you and others working with and for them?

Examples that people sometimes come up with are:

- being able to access the service immediately
- having all their needs met in one place
- having a tailored service based on their unique needs.

You will have your own factors for your beneficiaries. Once you've picked the top two, draw up a matrix showing each factor:

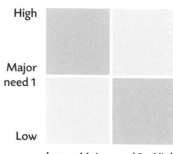

4. Plot out each of the other players and your own organisation on the matrix. You could draw a circle for each that gives an idea of relative size.

- Where are the gaps?
- Why are the gaps there?
- Who should be filling them? What potential is there for funding to create new services to meet need?
- How might you work with other players to better meet need?
- Where are the overlaps?
- What are the options for change?
- What are your options?
- What factors will affect your choice/decision making?
- What further research do you need to make?

Environmental analysis

Strategic group mapping Illustration

In this illustration, the two most important service factors in the market are 'immediate access' to services and that when accessed, the services are 'tailored' to meet individual need.

There are four key players in the locality, all working with the same group.

- United Services is the biggest player and provides a range of services. These services are not open access, but some services can be accessed with one of two days' notice, by appointment. Key workers try to make the service as tailored as possible but are pushed for time and really only have generic solutions, much of which are on a group work basis.
- Medway is a medium-sized player and has been around for many years, providing a set service by appointment only. All its work is on local authority contracts.

- Church Pastoral operates an open-door policy, but no tailored services; it is welcoming, but when you arrive you get what it has available.
- 'Us' – we are very clear about the need for bespoke services and have key workers assigned to each client, who work out a personalised package; we have a long waiting list, are oversubscribed and do not know where next year's funding will come from given the economic climate (most of our money comes from donations and small grants).

Commentary
- There is a big gap between what service users want and what is on offer from the local voluntary and community sector.
- Statutory funding does not at present cover the 'expensive' area of service provision: tailored service at the time it is needed.

- All players should be thinking about long-term sustainability – particularly Medway; if the local authority switches to a contract base for funding (which they will), Medway may not be delivering the outcomes/value required.
- United Services' plans may have a major impact on the market – what will their strategic plan be?

Some options
- There might be opportunity to use charitable monies to fund a time-limited small project on a temporary basis to pilot service provision in the immediate access/ tailored service arena (top right in the diagram); measure outcomes and impact, use this as a justification when lobbying for change with the local authority.
- There could be opportunity for other players to join in this pilot – to share skills and expertise: 'we' have skills in providing tailored services, Church Pastoral is brilliant at immediate access, United Services has infrastructure capacity to co-manage the work.
- Other players would benefit from understanding what United Services' strategic plans are; if they want to develop their service base, then any of the three other players might be interesting as merger candidates, perhaps particularly Medway.

Example of a strategic group map

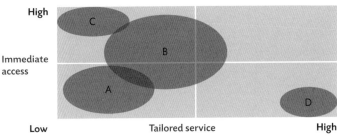

A. Medway   B. United Services   C. Church Pastoral   D. Us

2.8 Risk analysis Tool

What is it?

A risk analysis helps you list, sort, score and rank identified risks. This then forms a basis for trustees and staff to make informed and responsible decisions about how to handle all the risks that the organisation may face.

Why should you use it?

Benefits It enables you to:

- categorise risk
- prioritise risk
- assess the impact of risk.

Limitations It is only effective when placed in a total risk framework that also incorporates risk management; can be subjective.

When should you use it?

★ **Vital** as a tool to assess the environment from the risk perspective on an annual basis. It is one of the means by which management can fulfil their obligations of protecting and preserving the organisation and advising the board.

How to use the tool

Risk analysis involves listing all the potential risks that the organisation faces, then sifting and sorting the mass of information. The following steps will help you do this.

- **Devise:** headings and categories for all the risk areas to stimulate thinking, for example, finance, human resources, legislation, operations and reputation. Wordstorm the potential risks under each heading.
- **Review:** does the list accurately define the risks and their root causes? Simplify overly long lists by asking: are any of these items multiple symptoms of a bigger underlying issue and if so what is the root cause?
- **Score:** assess the risks to gauge their impact and likelihood; these can be designated as high, medium or low.

Risk map

Once the risks are scored they can then be plotted on to a risk map, which illustrates whether there is a potentially serious situation that requires urgent action, as well as less urgent issues. A risk map helps the organisation to decide its strategy for addressing risk and its priorities for action. Consider the following questions.

- What are the implications of the findings?
- What needs urgent attention, ie items that are high likelihood, high impact?
- What can we influence, what must we accommodate?
- Are there trade-offs we must make?
- How should we best allocate our resources?
- What strategies should we adopt to tackle each of the risks? Draw up a plan of action to influence, adapt, accommodate or exploit the situation.

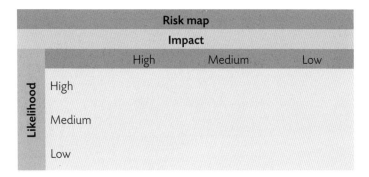

Risk map			
	Impact		
	High	Medium	Low
Likelihood High			
Medium			
Low			

Environmental analysis

Risk analysis
Illustration

This illustration is taken from an analysis carried out by a very small charity based in the UK but operating overseas.

The staff team and trustees met for a day and wordstormed all of the potential risks facing the organisation using a set of headings to stimulate their thinking:

- changes in the external environment (including policy and legislation)
- impact on reputation
- capacity (including human resources)
- control
- management practice (including operations)
- finance.

They then ranked the risks according to their impact and likelihood, and came up with the risk map below.

This focused their ideas about where to allocate their limited resources.

		Impact		
		High	**Medium**	**Low**
Likelihood	**High**	• Work is with children, so reputation affected when things go wrong. • Lack of capacity for fundraising; reserves very low. • No treasurer and no financial control.	• Missing opportunities to follow up partnership building leads means no investment for the future. • Board has no processes for monitoring and controlling what goes on. • Organisation only employs one staff member and is reliant on volunteers for cover. • Board devolves too much strategy development and decision making.	• Changes to charity legislation. • Changes in UK government legislation and overseas funding and policy. • Ageing players (eg trustees and volunteers).
	Medium	• Overseas partners may not deliver, affecting the integrity of our brand/ reputation. • Lack of information for decision making may mean we make the wrong ones. • Expertise in our line of work is increasingly hard to find.	• Lack of control over practice of overseas partners. • Overseas partners may just take from the relationship, not give. • Some partners have unrealistic expectations of us that we can't deliver on. • We could be charged more for our office space.	
	Low	• We could be kicked out of our current offices. • Responsibility for police checks devolved to overseas agencies.	• Finding new trustees is very difficult.	

2.9 Ansoff matrix
Tool

What is it?

An Ansoff matrix is a tool to help you decide how and where to expand your activities.

Why should you use it?

Benefits It helps you to identify your full range of choices for expansion in a customer-/market-focused way. In combination with SWOT it also helps you to choose between different strategic options and indicates a relative ranking of risk between the options.

Limitations It doesn't make the choices for you.

When should you use it?

Useful to use to supplement SWOT and other player analysis to help you get the facts to make a choice when your organisation has the capacity to expand and/or when you suspect it isn't using the full or right range of products/offerings.

How to use the tool

Identify all your current products/offerings and their markets, then consider your future options for expansion using the matrix below, considering opportunities, associated costs, benefits and risks.

Exploring the options
- The lowest risk option is to sell more of your existing offering in your existing market either by existing customers purchasing more or by increasing the number of customers from your existing market – the bottom left quadrant. This is increasing your market penetration.
- Somewhat more risky is to sell your existing product into new markets (more customers) – the top left quadrant. This is market development.
- More risky still is to develop new offerings for your existing markets – bottom right quadrant. This is product development.
- Most risky is to develop new offerings for new markets, called diversification – top right quadrant.

- If we introduce the charity dimension, these risk ratings might change, for example, if the existing offering is loss making, increasing the market penetration of a loss-making offering could be more risky than developing a new or amended product that breaks even.
- If your organisation has many offerings then it is useful to prioritise among them before applying the matrix, for example, start with the most important offerings as defined by fit with mission, volume of delivery, conclusions from SWOT and other player analysis.
- Unless there are particular reasons not to, start by exploring the lower risk options.
- Because of our sector's commitment to innovation we often neglect the two left quadrants, so make sure you explore these carefully.

Increasing market innovation ↑	Expanding through **existing** products into **new** markets (Development)	Expanding through **new** products into **new** markets (Diversification)
	Expanding through **existing** products in **existing** markets (Penetration)	Expanding through **new** products into **existing** markets (Product development)

Increasing product/offering innovation →

Environmental analysis

Ansoff matrix
Illustration

Introduction

Several major charities have large and
fairly sophisticated telephone
fundraising units. This is an analysis of
one of these using the Ansoff matrix.

Existing product into new markets

Having saturated the general public at home, the
next step was to sell into companies, ie an existing
product into a new market. The conversion rates
here were less successful and this was discontinued.

New offering into new markets

The new market of companies for raffle ticket sales
was less than successful. The charity then trialled a
new product for this new market – recycling ink
cartridges from computer and photocopying
equipment. This required a volunteer within the
company to return the cartridges to an address that
did the recycling. This proved a successful new
product launch into a new market.

Expanding existing offerings to existing market

Originally the charity sold books of raffle tickets
through its local fundraisers across the UK. After a
year or two, sales reached a plateau and it decided
to recruit a telephone 'sales' force which would also
sell the raffle tickets. Both the local fundraisers and
the telesales people were selling to the same general
market, ie the general public, but the telesales
fundraising method allowed a massive expansion of
the numbers of people reached.

Eventually, with millions of people being telephoned
each year, the maximum penetration of potential
raffle ticket purchasers from the general public at
home had been reached. The charity then modified
the offering to increase the number of tickets in
each of the raffle books by 20 per cent. Once again,
this second method to expand an existing product
in an existing market was successful.

New offerings into the existing market

Given that raffle ticket sales to the general public at
home were now virtually saturated, the charity
trialled a new product into the home – a small
cardboard collecting box for the family's and their
friends' spare change. This was a new product into
an existing market. This was successful and did not
seem to result in lowering the same household's
commitment to raffle ticket sales.

Increasing market innovation

Increasing product/offering innovation

Stage 3
Options and choice

3.1 Strategic options   p37
3.2 Other player options   p38
3.3 Force-field analysis   p39
3.4 Cost-benefit analysis   p41
3.5 Break-even analysis   p43
3.6 Strategy screen   p46

Options and choice

You will emerge from the analysis of your internal and external environment with a range of ideas about potential future activities and options, and a list of things you could do (probably a long one). The tools in this section will help you to:

- get to grips with, refine and categorise the activities and turn vague ideas into options
- assess them to determine if the ideas are feasible and what the resource implications are
- prioritise the options and determine what the most important activities are – making a choice
- get the ideas ready for the next stage of building the activities into the plan for the coming year.

At all times you should keep your organisation's mission (and the key strategic objectives if they remain relevant) as a backdrop to analysis and decision making.

We haven't touched on the process of getting approval for your choice and future strategy; this will depend on how your organisation operates. If the board or management committee has been driving the planning process as we recommend, much of the preparatory work of getting approval will have been done.

Tools included in this section

Strategic options	p37
Other player options	p38
Force-field analysis	p39
Cost-benefit analysis	p41
Break-even analysis	p43
Strategy screen	p46

3.1 Strategic options Tool

What is it?

This is a workshop tool to help explore all possible options creatively. It gives a range of alternative future strategic options for different services, different activities or particular geographical areas.

Why should you use it?

Benefits It stimulates your thinking.

Limitations There may be more options that are not listed here.

When should you use it?

Useful once you've evaluated your internal and external environment and need to make some basic choices about where you go next; consider using this about every three years (perhaps more frequently if you need to be responsive to change).

How to use the tool

Look through the range of options[1] below and think about those that are appropriate to your organisation. Weigh the pros and cons according to the results of your environmental analysis, always using your vision and mission as a backdrop.

All of the options could apply to services to a particular client group, individual services/activities (no matter what the client group) or all services in a particular geographical area. You could choose a different strategy for different services according to need.

Retrench Reduce, divest or close services/activities or work in geographical areas.	**Reduce costs** Reduce costs for a particular service/activity or in a geographical area.	**Maintain** Continue services/ activities as they are.	**Improve quality** Improve the quality of services/activities (maybe in a key geographical area).
Experiment Pilot services to a new client group or in a new geographical area, or pilot a new kind of service.	**Quantitative expansion** Increase the numbers of clients or the extent of provision.	**Expand boundary** Expand boundary of a particular client group, the amount of service provided or the boundary of the geographical area.	**New related strategy** Switch services to a related client group, type of service or geographical area.
Switch strategy A radical change to switch services totally to an unrelated client group, type of service or geographical area.	**Piggybacking** Develop fee-earning services to subsidise other activities – cross subsidy of activities.	**Collaborating** Develop a closer partnership with another agency in relation to a particular client group, service or geographical area.	**Unrelated expansion** Expand to add services to an unrelated client group, to an unrelated type of service or in an unrelated area.

[1] Adapted from Courtney R. (2002) Strategic Management for Voluntary Non Profit Organisations. London: Routledge. p207.

Options and choice

3.2 Other player options
Tool

What is it?

This is a follow-on from the other player analysis; once you've worked out who else is in your market and found some information about them, this will help you to consider the kind of relationship to develop with them.

Why should you use it?

Benefits It helps to prevent narrow thinking about the options for 'partnership working'.

Limitations It only helps to open up thinking; it doesn't provide any answers.

When should you use it?

 Vital to help consider what relationship you want with other players. It stresses the

importance of organisation 'self-awareness' and awareness of the market place, so should follow detailed environmental analysis.

How to use the tool

Think through the other players in your market and consider the different kinds of relationship you could have with them, using the matrix of options below as a prompt. You can pursue more than one option at the same time.

Some pointers about cooperation and collaboration

1. Be clear about your position, what you want and what's in it for you, them and your beneficiaries – think about how the other player's strategy will deliver your mission, play to your strengths and help you to overcome your weaknesses.

2. Open up a dialogue and find out what kind of relationship they want (they may want to do nothing for now).

3. Determine how well you could work together – chemistry and instinct play an important part. You don't have to be the same but you need to be compatible (in approach, culture/values, agenda/ priorities and between leaders and opinion formers).

4. Carry out a feasibility study, cost-benefit analysis and risk assessment if resources need to be invested.

5. Constantly reassess and have an exit strategy.

Compete	Do nothing	Cooperate/Complement
Take action to succeed (eg in bids, contracts) at the expense of another.	Take no action for now (but keep an eye on developments).	Establish informal relationships to mutual benefit.
Competing can dissipate resources, but it can also force efficiencies and improved quality: compete on cost or quality, or be different.	Strategies to work together or compete take time and resources; don't do it just for the sake of it or if you have other more pressing priorities.	Share information, resources, research, training, facilities, skills and second staff. Provide guidance and support. Look after each other's position.
Collaborate	**Merge**	**Takeover**
Establish more formal relationships to mutual benefit..	Transfer all activities from two into one merged organisation.	Absorb or assimilate another organisation.
A documented, legal agreement to share costs, risks and liabilities of a joint venture: service, project, post, trading subsidiary, resources, facilities and purchasing.	Creating one new legal entity to replace the two separate ones, where there is an equal opportunity to participate, with shared power and decision making.	Where the driving force is one organisation, sometimes one is in crisis. Usually one is more powerful and the other loses its identity.

3.3 Force-field analysis
Tool

What is it?

Force-field analysis is a tool to help you identify the forces working for and against a particular option, then help you analyse the things that will facilitate or block change. It's particularly helpful as a workshop tool.

Why should you use it?

Benefits It helps you decide whether a change or option is a good idea. If you have to undergo a particular change, it helps you work out what you need to consider when planning your actions.

Limitations Sometimes forces can both block and facilitate, depending on the circumstances.

When should you use it?

● **Useful** when you're considering any option, change or problem.

How to use the tool

Once you've defined the change you want to explore, draw up a able as shown below and list the positive and negative forces working for and against the change. This kind of analysis tool is always best used in a group.

Steps

1. Define precisely the change or option you want to test out.

2. List the forces for and against the change or option; sometimes it's hard to think of anything other than problems – use this to think about forces also working in your favour.

3. The forces need not be just about people – all features of your organisation that have an impact should be included, such as systems, processes, the culture, structures, nature of services and features of how you work.

4. If you come across forces that could be either positive or negative, try to pull out the elements that are positive and those that are negative.

5. Identify the forces that you cannot resist.

6. Rank the forces according to impact.

7. Think about what actions you can take to accentuate the positive and eliminate (or mitigate the effect of) the negative.

8. Decide whether you want to proceed with the option, and what you have to do to make it work; it's not just a strategy tool but also a general change management tool.

Summarise the change or option
Once you've listed the forces at work, you can weigh or rank them to show potential impact; those with a big impact can be tackled as a priority.

Positive forces: facilitating →	← Negative forces: blocking

Force-field analysis
Illustration

This section outlines the first listing that emerged from a workshop with a resource centre team in Yorkshire.

Just getting these issues on the table has already helped to form some early arguments. The next steps will be to refine the analysis and start to weigh some of the issues – boil it down to the big issues and make a decision about whether to invest in a proper feasibility study.

Setting up a new resource centre in Lancashire

Positive forces: support	Negative forces: inhibit
• We have the expertise in running a resource centre and are proud of our impact.	• None of our existing staff would be prepared to move to work in the new place; we'd have to recruit from scratch.
• We've learnt how to develop a high standard of care and should now be able to replicate the model at a much lower cost with lower risks.	• Early estimates show it will take four years to break even.
• Replicating the service in Lancashire would fit with our long-term vision of having a resource centre in every major city in the north-west of England.	• We would need to make sure that we didn't over stretch our management team if we have to manage across the two counties.
• We know that existing service users in Yorkshire need it and value it.	• We don't know the area or key players well and would need to develop our networks very quickly.
• Trustees will give us a small amount of money to do more research.	• Capital costs are high; we need to get funders to commit to help us with the initial investment.
• Initial conversations with potential funders show they are interested and at least acknowledge the need.	• Trustees are reluctant to invest charitable funds in capital costs.
• Maybe Megan House could help us in some way – if we could somehow persuade it we're not a threat.	• Megan House already provides some of the services in the area on an outreach basis and is very well connected – how would it see our arrival?
• The resource centre in Yorkshire has just broken even two years before our forecast, so we know it is a viable concern.	
• Initial market research shows large numbers of potential clients with patchy levels of service at present from a number of different service providers (no sign of any organisation offering a one-stop shop as we do).	

3.4 Cost-benefit analysis Tool

What is it?

A cost-benefit analysis is an evaluation technique used when the benefits of a project are intangible, even though costs may be known. It is based on the principle that market forces do not capture all costs and benefits, which is a potentially attractive concept in our sector.

Why should you use it?

Benefits Social benefits are analysed in detail and a value can be ascertained for social costs. This technique is understood and used in the public sector.

Limitations It requires a value judgement on costs. Its lack of scientific rigour means that it is distrusted by the private sector.

When should you use it?

● **Useful** when assessing a strategic option when benefits are intangible and funding is sought from public authorities.

How to use the tool

The net benefits for the project are estimated and then compared with costs. The project can be appraised by using discounted cash flow, which is explained below.

How to value intangible costs and benefits

There is a need to value in some way those intangible costs and benefits for which no market value exists in the first place. Although there is no completely satisfactory way of doing this, several approaches of 'surrogate pricing' have been suggested; these include:

● finding out what consumers would be willing to pay
● observing existing behaviour and then applying a valuation – for example, using volunteers and placing a value on those activities
● tracing the effects of a programme as far as possible and then trying to place a value on the costs and benefits of each effect.

Choosing a discount rate

Where costs and benefits occur at different points in time it will be necessary to discount them to some common time period before they can be realistically compared. For cost-benefit analysis the social discount rate is used but there is no agreement over how such a rate is derived. The following techniques have been suggested:

● social time preference rate (STPR) attempts to express the social discount rate as a rate that reflects society's preference for present benefits over future benefits; however, this technique is criticised as it leads to short-term decision making as individuals underestimate benefits in the future

● social opportunity cost rate (SOCR) works on the principle that as resources are limited, their use is not available elsewhere; an appropriate 'opportunity cost' is applied, for example, to interest forgone on an investment if left in the private sector, or the cost of borrowing.

Problems and issues

In reality, any discount rate that is chosen will suffer from some imperfection. Whether a real discount rate is assessed in some way or market rates are used, they will always be lacking in theoretical foundation. The important thing to remember is that like should always be discounted by like. So if a real discount rate is used, the costs and benefits should also be in real terms.

Cost-effectiveness analysis

It is because social costs and benefits are not easily measurable that cost-effectiveness analysis is used. Cost-effectiveness analysis involves a careful appraisal of the quantifiable costs and benefits, both now and in the future, of undertaking a project, with the non-quantifiable effects described but not evaluated. In other words, measuring the measurable – the following illustration demonstrates the practical difficulties associated with selecting discount rates.

Options and choice

Cost-benefit analysis
Illustration

A primary health care trust is considering whether to replace the current ambulance service, which takes disabled people from their home to hospital, with a local taxi firm or by funding a local Age Concern organisation that has proposed a community transport scheme using volunteers, with some paid professional drivers. The options are:

1. fund the purchase of minibuses with lift ramps and wheelchair space in the design – the initial cost would be £500,000, with operating costs of £180,000 per annum

2. provide vouchers to eligible passengers to use a local private taxi firm, which has a number of specially adapted taxis for disabled passengers, for a specified number of journeys per year – this would cost £250,000 per annum.

The life of the vehicles is five years and the authority has to apply a cost of capital rate of 7 per cent.

Based on the present value and simple cost analysis, option 2 would be the preferred choice but, as one authority member notes, taxi drivers just drive, while the community transport volunteers offer additional personal services and friendship. Should they value this benefit?

The trust could value these social benefits by:

- valuing the work of the volunteers
- using a higher discount factor to incorporate the social benefits.

Valuing volunteers
There are three cited methods to value volunteering:

1. the minimum wage method

2. the standard average wage method

3. the equivalent wage method.

The first two are easily calculated from government sources, representing the stated minimum wage and the average wage in the UK, but both are disliked as they undervalue volunteering. The equivalent method involves:

1. evaluating the job title

2. calculating true equivalent cost

3. calculating equivalent hours worked

4. calculating equivalent days off

5. calculating equivalent hourly rate.

The trust could now value the volunteer input and take this away from the costs of providing the service; however, it chooses a higher discount factor of 10 per cent on option 1 to reflect the intangible and social benefits.

Using a higher discount to allow for the social benefits, option 1 becomes the preferred decision. The exercise illustrates the problems of applying appropriate factors and why their choice must be applied rationally and fairly.

	Cash inflow £	Discount factor 7%	Present value £
Option 1 Years 1–5	500,000 180,000	0.713 4.100	356,500 738,000
Total cost			1,094,500
Option 2	250,000	4.100	1,025,000

Revised Option 1 at 10 per cent discount factor

	Cash inflow £	Discount factor 10%	Present value £
Option 1 Years 1–5	500,000 180,000	0.621 3.790	310,500 682,200
Total cost			992,700
Option 2 Years 1–5	250,000	7% 4.100	1,025,000

3.5 Break-even analysis
Tool

What is it?

This is a technique for analysing the relationship between costs and volume, to establish at what point the two are in equilibrium and the initial investment is recouped. It is also known as cost-volume-profit analysis.

Why should you use it?

Benefits It gives useful insights for short-term decision making.

Limitations It's difficult to allocate the correct amount of fixed costs to a particular service and identify exactly the variable costs.

When should you use it?

⬤ **Useful** when you are assessing a strategic option with income based on usage and need to know at what point the income will cover the costs.

How to use the tool

Understanding costs
The basic principle of cost behaviour is that as a level of activity rises, costs will usually rise. The problem is that you also need to understand in what ways costs rise, and by how much, as the level of output increases.

Fixed and variable costs
Fixed costs do not change with outputs, for example, rental of a telephone line. Variable costs do vary with level of output, for example, telephone charges for the duration of the call.

The contribution concept
This is the most useful feature of break-even analysis – the contribution is the difference between income and variable costs. The contribution first covers the fixed cost then, after the break-even point, provides a surplus.

Formula
The following formula shows how to calculate the break-even point:

Break-even point =

$$\frac{\text{Fixed costs}}{\text{Contribution per unit}}$$

Worked example: calculating the break-even point
A local authority fee of £25 finances an advice service for every client seen. There are certain fixed costs. It would be useful to know how many clients have to be seen each month for the service to break even. Costs can be viewed in the table below.

Calculating the contribution
Contract income (local authority fee) less variable costs = contribution ($£25-£5 = £20$)

The contribution is so called because it literally contributes towards the fixed costs, which are incurred no matter how many people are seen. Therefore, if the advice service sees one person there is a £20 contribution towards the fixed costs of £800. If there are two people, there is a £40 contribution towards the fixed costs of £800, and so on.

To break even, the advice service needs sufficient contributions to pay all the fixed costs. The service will then have nothing left (no surplus and no deficit); the break-even point will have been reached. So, £800/£20 = 40 people per month to break even.

Fixed costs	£ per month
Rent and rates	200
Salaries	500
Telephone rental	100
Total	800

Variable costs	£ per person (average)
Telephone calls	4
Refreshment	1
Total	5

Options and choice

Break-even analysis
Illustration

A community centre has to decide whether to accept a 'fixed-price' contract with the local authority to operate a community kitchen. One key factor in the decision will be: how many homeless people does the community centre need to attract in order to break even each month?

The estimates of monthly costs can be seen in the table below.

Fixed costs	£ per month
Rent and rates	800
Salaries	1,500
Insurance	100
Other	100
Total	2,500
Variable costs	**£ per person (average)**
Food and drink	3
Laundry	1
Other	1
Total	5

The contract with the local authority will provide a fixed fee of £10 for every homeless person fed. It is now possible to calculate the break-even point. The first step is to calculate the contribution from each person.

Every time the community centre serves a homeless person it receives £10 and has to pay £5 for food, etc.

The management accounting term for this difference of £5 is the 'contribution'. Therefore the community centre gets a contribution of £5 per person:

Contract income less variable cost = contribution (£10−£5 = £5)

The contribution is so called because it literally contributes towards the fixed costs that are incurred no matter how many people are served. Therefore if the community centre has one homeless person walk in, there is a £5 contribution towards the fixed costs of £2,500, and so on.

To break even, the community centre needs sufficient contributions to pay all the fixed costs. The centre will then have nothing left (no surplus and no deficit); the break-even point will have been reached.

Break-even point =

$$\frac{\text{Fixed costs} \qquad £2,500}{\text{Contribution per person} \qquad £5}$$

Break-even point is 500 people per month.

If the community centre were to serve more than 500 people then it would start to make a surplus of £5 per person. This can be illustrated by a break-even chart. The break-even chart consists of five straight lines. The first two lines are known as the axes:

1. the horizontal axis, which represents 'number', in this case meals sold

2. the vertical axis, which represents 'money', either income or expenditure.

The other three lines represent various factors in the calculation:

3. a horizontal line, which represents the fixed cost

4. a line that represents the variable costs for different quantities of consumption, and which slopes upwards from where the fixed cost line crosses the vertical axis

5. a line that represents the total income from different quantities (meals consumed) and slopes upwards from the origin.

The community centre's break-even chart and contribution concept

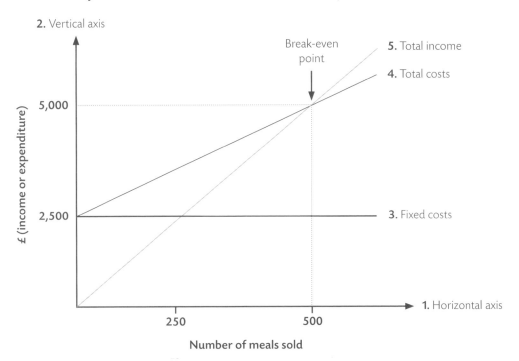

Options and choice

3.6 Strategy screen Tool

What is it?

The strategy screen is a set of decision-making criteria against which you can test or screen various options that are contenders to be included in your future strategy.

Why should you use it?

Benefits It gives you the most objective basis possible for decision making and encourages analysis and comparison of options.

Limitations When faced with the reality of the situation, people's views can change. Sometimes a certain situation is unavoidable, but at least this 'discipline' will encourage some in-depth consideration of the options.

When should you use it?

★ **Vital** when boards and management teams need to be clear about the basis of their strategic decisions. It's healthy to agree the criteria before you have to make a choice (although it is also important to be pragmatic). Even if there are no other options, it's good to know the strengths and weaknesses of the actions so you can plan to minimise the impact.

How to use the tool

Work with your board and leadership team to wordstorm their decision-making criteria and rank these in order of importance to the group. Screen your different strategic options against these, scoring each option according to the criteria, perhaps on a scale of 1–5, where 5 is high.

The table below contains an illustration of the tool (note that each organisation will have their own criteria).

Decision-making criteria	Option 1	Option 2	Option 3
Fit with mission, vision and values			
Impact on beneficiary			
Filling known gap			
Are we best placed to do this? (Can no one else do it better?)			
Impact of change agenda on organisation (structure, etc)			
Your capacity to pursue (consider investment, other effort etc)			
Risk to reputation (severity and likelihood)			
Level of support for the option (internal and external)			
Break-even point (in years)			
Sustainability (years to receive payback after break even)			
Ability to generate cash			
Ability to generate a quick win			

Stage 4
Planning

4.1 Goal and target setting   p49
4.2 Writing a strategic plan   p50
4.3 Budgeting   p51

Planning

The tools in the previous section will have helped you generate options and sift/sort activities to be included in future plans. By now your favoured set of options and activities will have emerged and a choice been made. At this point you need to start the process of turning broad ideas about the future into reality, building the new work into everyday activities. To do this you can develop some goals and targets, capture the strategy in some kind of written document and think about the resources required to deliver the plan. This section includes some good practice guides covering all of the above.

It is important that the broad analysis and reasons for the choice of future strategy are documented, not least because the starting point and assumptions need to be clear to everyone. We are not advocating writing a plan for the sake of it, but to add to the bank of knowledge of your organisation. We do not recommend the production of weighty tomes; some of the best plans are written on the backs of envelopes and stuck on the wall so that everyone can read, adapt and apply them. At their worst, plans are long, dusty, perfectly laid out and bound documents, sitting on shelves never to be referred to again. Plans should pass the 'battered corner' test!

We have included a section on budgeting, but in the sense of a budget being an expression of the plan in financial terms. The good practice guide on budgeting is just the tip of the iceberg in terms of the thinking that you will need to do about setting a budget, so we have indicated where you can find more information in the signpost section towards the end of the toolkit.

Good practice guides included in this section

Goal and target setting p49
Writing a strategic plan p50
Budgeting p51

4.1 Goal and target setting
Good practice guide

What is it?

This is a process of making lists of actions, which together will ensure delivery of your organisation's strategy. These are linked at all levels so that the energy of individuals and teams is channelled into the critical areas.

Why should you use it?

Benefits It achieves coherent thrust and avoids gaps and clashes.

Limitations If targets are imposed without consultation, individuals will be less committed to using them.

When should you use it?

 Useful once you've decided on your strategy for the future.

Organisation and team goals: set these at least annually.

Individual targets: usually set these quarterly.

How to use the guide

Draw up goals and targets as a series of interlocking steps, involving the appropriate people at each level.

To monitor your progress, you should create SMART goals that are:

- **S**pecific
- **M**easureable
- **A**chievable
- **R**ealistic
- **T**ime based.

It's important that a team member can link their work with the overall strategic objectives of the organisation.

The interlocking steps can be seen in the table below.

Step 1 Set strategic objectives	Step 2 Set annual goals	Step 3 Set key performance indicators (KPIs)	Step 4 Set targets
Objectives for the organisation as a whole, rather than for specific departments; to cover all of the areas of activity for the organisation.	Some may be specific to one department, but increasingly goals will be tackled by project teams drawn from several areas. Together the goals will deliver the strategic objectives for the coming year and can be used as one of the baselines for evaluating progress. They should be short sharp actions that focus on current priorities.	KPIs highlight the individual's most important ongoing accountabilities and can be the focus of performance management discussions.	Managers with individual team members.
Involve trustees and senior management team (SMT). Expected duration: three years.	Involve SMT with managers/team leaders. Duration: one year.	Involve managers with individual team members. Duration: until further notice.	Duration: short term – a few months.

4.2 Writing a strategic plan
Good practice guide

What is it?

This is a document to capture the organisation's strategy. Strategic plans can be given different names, but they will include the following characteristics:

- usually cover a planning period of three to five years
- often summarised in an executive summary
- will have a 'budget' or funding strategy attached, which will show the resources required to fulfil the plan, at a high level
- the first year of the plan may be covered in more detail in an 'annual operating plan', with detailed budgets.

Why should you use it?

Benefits Everyone gets a consistent view of what needs to happen and why.

Limitations It's easy for a plan to become the end itself, rather than the means to the end.

When should you use it?

★ **Vital** once the analysis and choice of strategic options has been made, and the future direction is known.

How to use the guide

Use the headings below as a guide to structuring your plan contents; collect and sort the analysis generated so far in your strategic planning tasks.

Executive summary	A summary of the plan – you may wish to make this summary something you can promote outside the organisation, to build support and keep stakeholders informed.
Introduction	The purpose of the plan; background about where the organisation is in its development; brief statistics about numbers of staff/volunteers; a description of service users (snapshot).
Purpose	Cover the (new) mission, vision and values for the organisation – this is the backdrop for the plan; say how you use these important statements.
Drawing from the past	Set out learning from the past – about beneficiary need, about your organisation's performance, what you must continue to do; set some context for the plan.
Future potential	Outline what the challenges are for the future (external opportunities, threats, other player potential, stakeholder needs, etc); outline your fitness to face this future (the results of your internal environment analysis).
Strategic objectives for the next three years	Cover the main areas of work the organisation needs to focus on for the next three years – each objective should have key tasks and outcome measures associated with it, from which you can develop annual goals, and teams and individuals can develop their work plans.
Delivering the plan and timetable	This is where you need to be convincing about the organisation's ability to resource the plan – outline the high level activities over the period; attach a budget and a timetable to show when and how the strategic objectives will be met (covering all of the main areas of work of the organisation).

4.3 Budgeting
Good practice guide

What is it?

This is a guide to the key decisions you need to think about when drawing up a budget. A budget is a plan translated into money for a defined period (usually one year). The budget is prepared after you've clarified your strategic objectives and annual goals, and produced a variety of action plans to achieve them.

Why should you use it?

Benefits Enables you to:

- communicate and set financial targets
- maximise and allocate resources
- identify financial problems
- establish a system of control.

Limitations Can dominate and restrict thinking and decision making.

When should you use it?

Vital part of the planning process once you've determined your strategic objectives and annual goals. The budget process translates plans into pounds.

Planning

Budgeting
Good practice guide

How to use the guide

Before you calculate the budget, a
number of key activities will need to
take place. These are outlined below.

Forecasts	This requires each budget area to ask questions such as 'It cost this much last year, how much will it cost this year?' and the gathering of more complex information gleaned from other parts of the planning process.
Reviews	Many budgets are drawn up yearly by applying a percentage increase. This incremental budgeting fails to consider whether costs and activities are still relevant and appropriate. Thus mistakes from one year can too easily be carried forward to the next. Avoid this with regular reviews of your activities.
Evolving adjustments	During the year events can occur that cause or require change, resulting in budgets becoming unrealistic. Budgets have to reflect these new circumstances, otherwise they will signal or obscure a problem that has been or needs to be resolved.
Clarify who is accountable	The planning process will have clarified who has the power to affect various parts of the budget. They are then allocated responsibility and become the budget holder.
Set clear timescales	Budgets must be completed to a deadline. Realistic dates need to be set to allow those contributing to the budget and those doing the calculations sufficient time to complete their tasks. The timing must also match the decision-making process of funders.
Scheduling	Budgeting is a cyclical activity that must be built into the organisation's annual diary. It should begin six months before the new budget year.
Technical support	This requires the finance officer (or relevant person) to send out a budget worksheet, which is completed by budget holders; the finance officer is then able to turn the worksheets into budgets, which can be discussed and approved.
Take decisions	You must decide whether to set a balanced budget (one that produces neither surplus nor loss) or a deficit or surplus one.
Budgetary control	The finance team (or other nominated person) must provide timely reports comparing actual results against the current year. (From these, the manager responsible can take corrective action if needed.) This information forms the foundation for the new budget.
Variance reports	The most important aspect of control is variance analysis, which involves the comparison of actual results with budgeted expectations: the difference is the variance and is useful in planning the new budget.
Exception reports	Use exception reports to explain large variances. Small variances should be expected, so avoid overwhelming people with unnecessary information.

Stage 5
Implementation

5.1 Change management   p55
5.2 Performance management p56
5.3 Project management   p57

Implementation

The saddest strategy stories always seem to involve the 'Case of the Forgotten Plan'. People put a lot of effort into developing a strategy, and nothing ever changes. This section contains some good practice guides to help you embed new activities into everyday working life – a guide on some useful project management techniques, an outline of a performance management process and some tips on effective change management.

One of the most powerful elements of performance management is that, as well as focusing individual and team effort on the strategic objectives of the organisation, it also allows two-way feedback on overall direction. New ideas about future direction and strategy often emerge at the 'front line' of an organisation, particularly with people working directly with service users. You should ensure that your performance management processes encourage and capture emerging strategies as they are developed. Feedback loops enabling two-way communication between staff and managers/trustees need to be in place to ensure that there is coherence between the mission and what is happening at the front line of the organisation. Staff need to have a direct 'line of sight' between their role (and the impact they have) and the mission and overall impact of the organisation.

Good practice guides included in this section

Change management	p55
Performance management	p56
Project management	p57

5.1 Change management
Good practice guide

What is it?

This is a guide to two important concepts behind effective change management:

- understanding the necessary conditions for effective change
- the importance of having a vision-driven approach.

Why should you use it?

Benefits It offers a process to help when things get tough.

Limitations It's a huge challenge!

When should you use it?

 Vital if the change is going to affect people in any way.

Necessary conditions for effective change?[1]
Managers need to understand the following three conditions, and ensure that they are met.

Awareness: understanding and credibility are vital – people must know what their role is and understand the benefits of the change and its objectives, etc and they must have confidence in the likely success of the change to be energised to adapt their behaviour. **Will:** those involved need to value the outcomes of the change, they must feel able to choose to pursue the changes and they must choose to pursue and adopt them. Very often in our sector this will be about demonstrating the benefits of the change to service users. **Capability:** people must feel that they can cope, that they will be capable of being a part of the changed situation and that they can acquire the necessary skills and knowledge to work in the changed environment.

'People in change need empathy, information, ideas, milestones and feedback.'

How to use the guide

1. Determine the need for change, establish the purpose and reason for the change, and explain 'why'.

2. Define the desired future state, paint a vivid picture of what the change will look like when it's complete and what the benefits will be (particularly to service users or beneficiaries).

3. Describe the present state, taking care never to denigrate the past; be very clear about what needs to be changed in order to create the new future.

4. Create a transition plan to get from here to there, and give everyone a part to play in the transition (remember awareness, will and capability).

5. Celebrate – try to find some way of marking the passing of the old way as a psychological launch.

6. Manage through the transition state; this often needs real leadership – inspiring around the shared vision, experimenting, collaborating, strengthening, setting the example, and recognising achievements, learning and risk taking.

A vision-driven approach[2]

Present state	Transition state	Desired future state

---

[1] From Carnall C. (1999) Managing Change in Organisations. Harlow: Prentice Hall.

[2] Adapted from Beckhard R. and Harris R.T. (1987) Organizational Transitions – Managing Complex Change. Reading, MA: Addison Wesley.

Implementation

5.2 Performance management
Good practice guide

What is it?

This is a process for focusing individual and collective effort on agreed goals, reviewing progress and rewarding achievement.

Why should you use it?

Benefits It keeps people's attention concentrated on the most important issues.

Limitations Rewards for achievement may be skewed towards what is easiest to measure. This guide isn't intended for use when dealing with poorly performing staff.

When should you use it?

● **Useful** as part of strategy implementation and as a continuous cycle: set goals – take actions – assess results – reward achievement – set new goals.

How to use the guide

As part of the process of setting goals and targets (see the goal and target setting good practice guide), consider how and when progress will be measured. Measures can be of:

• input (use of resources)
• process (activities)
• output (work carried out)
• outcome (consequences of work done).

Financial measures may be obvious, but also consider other aspects such as the organisation's reputation, the sharing of knowledge and the talents and creativity of people.

Performance management guidelines

1. Performance management can cover both individual and team actions.

2. Some goals will be about completing a task over a set period, while others may be primarily about the personal development of an individual.

3. Regular progress reviews (at least four times a year) between the individual and their manager keep up momentum and allow fresh targets to be set and ideas for new developments to emerge and be included in future strategy.

4. A person's performance is the outcome of their ability (knowledge and skills) and their motivation (attitude, behaviour and confidence). Major improvements in performance usually derive from the latter.

5. An annual performance review should focus more on the future than on the past. Increasingly this involves people beyond the immediate manager: '360-degree feedback' can include the person's team members and colleagues as well as external sources such as service users.

6. Managers may need training and support in tackling poor performance. It's very demoralising for the majority of employees if a few individuals are allowed to 'escape' being challenged over lack of effort.

7. Salary review should be carried out at a different time of year from the annual performance review, because it will have to take into account factors beyond performance. The relationship between performance and pay should be transparent.

8. Reward does not have to be limited to pay; non-financial recognition can also be much valued by individuals.

5.3 Project management
Good practice guide

What is it?

This is a guide to two of the key project management tools – writing terms of reference and drawing up a Gantt chart.

Why should you use it?

Benefits It introduces some discipline into the organisation of a project.

Limitations Once published, people sometimes feel the documents can't be changed; they can, but changes should be tracked and logged.

When should you use it?

 Useful at the start of any project.

Terms of reference

Terms of reference define the context of the project and the goals and scope. Any subsequent deviation would need to be agreed and tracked.

Contents of terms of reference

Authority statement	Describes who has asked for the work to be carried out – who is the 'higher authority'.
Customer statement	Describes who the project is being done for – who the customer or final user is.
Purpose statement	Simple statement about why the organisation is doing the work – aligned with the mission or strategy of the organisation.
Scope statement	Puts boundaries on the project – to make clear what the project will and will not deliver; also states links to other projects/responsibilities.
Deliverables	What the project will produce.
Resource and schedule estimates	Realistic estimates.
Objectives and outcomes	Measurable criteria for success.
Risks and contingencies	Includes any significant risks or problems identified, along with associated contingency plans.
Stakeholders	All stakeholders should be listed, and their needs and expectations considered.

Gantt chart

This is a bar chart where time is shown on the horizontal axis and tasks or activities are shown on the vertical axis.

It shows what is being done, how long it is expected to take and when it's planned to happen. Some Gantt charts will also show who is responsible.

You can add a lot more information to a Gantt chart such as:

- tasks that are dependent upon each other
- tasks' milestones (key deliverables at the end of a task, or at a midpoint, such as a progress review)
- highlighting any 'slack' or 'burden' (periods of little or too much activity) in a plan. (Gantt charts are particularly useful at this, which makes them helpful for scheduling resources.)

Example of a Gantt chart

	January	February	March	April
Task 1	————			
Task 2		————		
Task 3			————	
Task 4		————————————————		

Stage 6
Evaluation

6.1 Assessment and reporting   p61
6.2 Outcome assessment   p62

Evaluation

This section includes two good practice guides to help you continue to evaluate the ongoing effectiveness of your strategy: a tool on general assessment and reporting, plus a tool to help you with outcome assessment.

Outcome assessment is the process by which we measure the impact of our work. It is an essential function of strategic planning, and one of those concepts that is disarmingly simple, indispensably valuable, prone to over-complication and too infrequently practised.

Outcome assessment means not only monitoring and evaluating the quality and quantity of outputs but also assessing the impact of those outputs. Too often, monitoring is seen as a matter of crunching numbers, ticking boxes and complying with funders' demands, and evaluation as something that happens at the end of a project as an endnote. By contrast, outcome assessment is a continual creative process; it sets out an early framework detailing where you are heading and what you are attempting to do, and establishes a point of reference for you to measure your progress and achievements.

There are a variety of ways in which organisations can begin to assess their outcomes, some of which are set out in this toolkit. It is essential that organisations adopt an outcome assessment method that is proportionate to the scale of their work and that is realistic about the challenges of attributing outcomes to their work. Its principles should be central to the entire strategic planning process.

By assessing what we achieve – as well as measuring what we do – on a continual basis throughout a project's lifecycle, we can judge how effective our outputs are at moving us towards the fulfilment of our strategic objectives. Accordingly, outcome assessment enables us to retain flexibility, learn continually and make improvements to our work as we travel. As such, it can be an incredibly energising and motivating process.

Moreover, funders are increasingly interested in funding mutually agreed outcomes rather than immediate outputs and, in return, prepared to be more flexible on the means by which outcomes are achieved. In place of monitoring and evaluation being imposed from outside, outcome assessment provides a framework for understanding and doing things better. Outcome assessment is our 'flexible friend'.

Good practice guides included in this section

Assessment and reporting p61
Outcome assessment p62

6.1 Assessment and reporting
Good practice guide

What is it?

This is a guide to help develop assessment and reporting processes to sustain strategic planning and activity. This will help you:

- stay on course and focus on what's important
- produce evidence of performance against your plan, to motivate and focus effort
- trigger contingency activities if things aren't going to plan
- remain flexible to changes affecting the organisation through the year, to ensure the strategy remains valid.

Why should you use it?

Benefits It fits in with the 'plan – do – review – re-plan' cycle introduced by other tools.

Limitations The diversity of the sector makes this a very general tool that you need to adapt.

When should you use it?

⬤ **Useful** as a guide when considering the implementation of a new strategic plan – the processes should be part of regular performance management.

How to use the guide

For each of the strategic objectives, annual goals or outcomes that provide the focus of your plan, establish some key indicators that can be used to monitor progress: we've called these milestones. On a quarterly basis gather performance data about what's actually happened, and present this assessment information.

Quarterly progress assessment and reporting against key milestones

Milestones are indicators of how you are progressing against the goal, objective or outcome – they are things that indicate whether something has happened or not, or if you are on track towards it. They can be quantitative (can be counted) or qualitative (an assessment can be made of people's experiences), and need to be established when you set the goal, objective or outcome. They can be adapted over time as experience dictates.

Questions to ask against each milestone

- Is what we are doing still relevant and appropriate? What new circumstances, issues and opportunities have emerged since we established the plan?
- How will we need to change the plan (and then objectives, goals, outcomes and their indicators) to reflect this?
- What's actually happened over the last quarter – what have we achieved, what hasn't happened? And again, how will we need to adapt the goals and indicators?
- How can we celebrate and share progress against the plan? Think about the audience and their needs (for example, newsletter, team meetings).
- How can we learn from what's happened, to improve performance next time?

	Milestone 1	M2	M3	M4	etc
Quarter 1	Progress				
Q2					
Q3					
Q4					

Evaluation

6.2 Outcome assessment
Good practice guide

What is it?

Outcome assessment is a process for assessing the changes that happen as a result of your work. Outcome assessment is about assessing effectiveness rather than efficiency.

Why should you use it?

Benefits It helps to demonstrate that your organisation is making a difference to your target group.

Limitations There is a danger that you focus only on intended outcomes and overlook the unintended ones.

When should you use it?

● **Useful** when defining strategic objectives, annual goals and targets. It's also useful when evaluating what has been achieved and what progress has been made. Increasingly, organisations are being asked to 'measure' their outcomes by funders. It is important that organisations address the challenge of outcome assessment before it is required of them externally, so that they are in a better situation to negotiate the terms of the assessment.

How to use the guide

1. The outcome assessment should be fully implemented across the organisation, creating a fully embedded culture of continuous improvement and shared organisational learning.

2. To assess change, it is necessary to collect the same information more than once.

3. Outcome assessment should look at final outcomes but also at distance travelled (the progress that has been made towards those final outcomes, such as improved self-confidence or the increased ability to work with others).

4. Time and costs needed to carry out the assessment should be budgeted for. A balance needs to be struck between the benefits of the assessment and its possible costs.

5. Assessment should be kept simple and be adapted to organisational objectives, context and capacity. With this in mind, it is important to be selective and realistic about the number and the kind of outcomes you want to assess.

6. Both qualitative and quantitative indicators of change should be included. Quantitative indicators rely on what is easily measurable, but in failing to address issues that cannot be quantified the organisation will fail to do justice to the organisation's full contribution.

7. Qualitative approaches (for example, individual and group interviews) are particularly useful to understand stakeholder perspectives and foster participation. They can also help to identify obstacles to success.

8. The results of the assessment should be fed back to stakeholders and acted upon to improve services.

Outcome assessment
Illustration

A six-month employment project

(Source: Sally Cupitt, Charities Evaluation Services)

Project aims

The employment project has four specific aims. It hopes to:

- increase users' lifestyle stability
- increase users' skills
- increase users' confidence and motivation
- enable users to find employment.

Project outcomes

Each of the employment project aims encompasses several outcomes. These describe a change for service users.

Aims	Outcomes
To increase users' lifestyle stability	Users get temporary accommodation Users get permanent accommodation Increased ability to budget Less chaotic lifestyle
To increase users' skills	Improved core skills Improved job-specific skills Improved job-search skills
To increase users' confidence and motivation	Users' confidence increases Users' motivation increases Users' aspirations change
To enable users to find employment	Users attend a work placement Users get paid work Users get voluntary work

Outcome indicators

These show that the outcome has happened, or that you are making progress towards it.

Examples of indicators for four of the outcomes are contained in the table opposite.

Outcomes	Indicators
Less chaotic lifestyle	Punctuality at service Stability of peer group Maintain/resume family relationships
Improved job-search skills	Whether user has a CV Whether user is able to identify suitable jobs in paper Ability to complete application form Reported level of interview skills Appropriateness of presentation
Users' confidence increases	Level of reported confidence Increased interaction with others Frequency user initiates contact with workers
Users attend a work placement	Whether user goes on a placement

Outcome monitoring framework

Deciding for each indicator the way the information will be collected (how, when and by whom).

Examples for four of the outcome indicators are contained in the table opposite.

Indicators	How	When	By whom
Punctuality at service	Attendance sheet	Daily	Project worker
Ability to complete application form	Observation	Weekly	Project worker
Level of reported confidence	Self-assessment questionnaire	Monthly	User
Whether user goes on a placement	Record-keeping	Weekly	Project worker

Resources

Communication and involvement tools p66
Books and web resources   p70
Further support   p76

Resources
Communication and involvement tools

For all the tools, we recommend involving a range of people in developing ideas and in impact analysis/decision making. You can maximise the effectiveness of your communication and involvement activities in a number of ways.

Use focus groups or workshops

- A focus group is a discussion of a nominated subject by selected participants who are facilitated to achieve an objective.
- Focus groups can be very helpful in developing ideas, exploring issues, developing solutions, carrying out impact analysis – all elements of strategic planning.
- Focus groups give people the opportunity to voice their opinions on critical matters, which is a crucial part of building their commitment to the end result.
- Focus groups are particularly effective in involving a cross-section of people, especially service users and beneficiaries.
- It is often helpful to agree a few ground rules at the start (for example, be brief rather than speak at length; speak for yourself; focus on the issue; focus on the positive).

Setting up the focus group

- Always use a facilitator, particularly if you need to be a player rather than a facilitator; find someone neutral to take on the role.
- The purpose of the session should be considered when deciding who should attend; try to invite people who will be affected or who represent those affected; use board members to help set the agenda.
- Organisation-wide issues should be discussed in cross-sectional focus groups; sometimes the process of getting a representative from every level of the organisation is called taking a 'diagonal slice'.
- The optimum size of a focus group is between 8 and 10 people.
- Participants should be given an incentive to attend and participate.
- The room needs to be set up so that everyone can see each other and the flip chart.
- Lots of pens/markers and paper should be made available; if you're doing 'snowballing' (see below), bring brown paper and stick it together and to the wall first (so that the results can be folded and kept).
- Think about using a note taker.

Encourage creativity

- Wordstorming is a quick way of getting ideas out of heads: have people shout out their ideas on a certain subject (be clear what the subject is) and write the ideas on a flip chart. Everyone should suspend censorship, evaluation and comment until stage two, when the group can start to sift, sort, rank and remove – again in open discussion or by voting.
- Snowballs are another way of wordstorming, where people write their ideas down on Post-it notes then stick them (on brown paper) on the wall. Once everyone has put their ideas up, the group can sift, sort, acknowledge similarities and differences, categorise, find patterns and generally build on the ideas. This is a very useful technique with people who are shy or initially reluctant to participate.
- Rounds are a more orderly form of group creative thinking, particularly useful when everyone should listen, give an idea or a view and have an equal opportunity to be heard (for example, if the subject is contentious and needs to be owned). The facilitator will go round the room encouraging everyone to give their idea/view on

a subject (there should be no debate, just giving of ideas/views), and writing down the idea/view on a flip chart. Each person should have an allotted time. Everyone should listen closely and try to build on others' ideas when it is their turn to speak. The facilitator should summarise by pulling out agreements and differences. The group should continue until a list of agreements emerges.

Build consensus – for decisions or for prioritisation
- Once a range of options or a series of proposals has emerged and a decision needs to be made, these are documented on flip chart paper (one option per sheet) and stuck on the wall.
- Each group member then marks the proposal closest to their own view (only one tick allowed).
- The options with no ticks are removed and all the votes are erased (ready for the next stage).
- Using rounds (see above) the facilitator asks each person to suggest a modification to an option, which would make it even closer to their view; the modification is made in a different coloured pen.

- Everyone votes again.
- As the group gets closer to agreement it may emerge that a small number of people are the dissenters – they should be asked to propose amendments that will make the option acceptable to everyone.
- In the case of a need to prioritise between options, the same approach can be taken, except that people can be given five stickers to vote with – they can attach all five to one option or spread their vote around. Top priorities will emerge.

Setting up an away day

An away day is a specific kind of focus group or workshop that is often used in the voluntary and community sector to kick-start the strategic planning process. The following steps should be followed.

Step	Example
1. Set an objective for the day; the objective will depend on where you are in the planning cycle. It would be helpful to consult with key internal stakeholders (trustees, members of the management team) about the scope of the day.	• If you have not revisited your mission for a few years and the external environment is changing, you may want to make your objective: 'To review our mission, and against this develop a picture of the key issues in our internal and external environment.'
2. Think about whether you need to use an external facilitator; if you do, now would be a good time to bring them in to help with thinking and process.	
3. Given the objective, think about who needs to be there, and therefore the best time/place to hold the meeting and the optimum length of the meeting, to ensure maximum attendance. While an away day is very useful to generate ideas about the issues or the content of plans, it would be unusual for it to be a decision-making forum. The board would usually expect outputs from an away day to be worked on by the chief executive and management team afterwards and recommendations brought back to a future board meeting for decision.	• If your organisation is small, you might want to invite everyone, otherwise a 'diagonal slice' of representatives from across the organisation (from trustees, staff and service users) might be helpful. • Some organisations choose the weekend for their away day, for example, if their trustees all have day jobs; some decide to make the venue outside the workplace to motivate and help build creativity. • It would be usual for the meeting to last a whole day, eg 10am until 4.30pm.
4. Check the timings with everyone who will attend; book the venue and tell about the meeting, its purpose, and why it's important for them to attend. Remember to think about ensuring inclusion and access – think about the needs of the group and how you might facilitate everyone's contribution.	

Step	Example
5. Again, depending on the objective, think through the range of tools you might use and how long you want/ need to give to each. Write the agenda and check that key internal stakeholders are happy with it. Distribute the agenda so that people can start thinking about their contribution.	• With the above sample objective you might choose from the toolkit: stakeholder analysis (you could have the management team and staff prepare a presentation in advance); mission, vision and values – perhaps just covering mission; a presentation from staff on PEST and internal health check, followed by a SWOT.
6. Think through how you will stimulate people to be creative and contribute (think about some of the techniques featured in the case studies in this toolkit). Try to vary your techniques, eg between small-group work, large-group work and exercises where people can work on	• With the above example, you might make stakeholder analysis a whole-team exercise; mission, vision and values a small-group exercise with summing up in the large group; the presentation followed by a SWOT a whole-group exercise. • Including lunch (particularly important!), this will probably take the whole day. Finish by agreeing next steps and a planning timetable.
7. On the day, get the room ready in advance (see the earlier notes on setting up a focus group), and don't forget ground rules. Remember to think about follow-up and feedback.	• If you are expecting people who are not used to focus groups and workshops, think about how you can organise things to make them feel comfortable and safe to take part; giving people something to do is often helpful.

Resources
Books and web resources

General books, journals and websites on strategy and planning	
Ross B. and Segal C. (2002) *Breakthrough Thinking for Non-profit Organizations*. San Francisco: Jossey-Bass.	Full of good examples from the voluntary and community sector, this book takes a refreshing look at different ways of thinking about strategy, change, creativity and innovation.
Courtney R. (2007) *Strategic Management for Voluntary Non-profit Organizations*. London: Routledge.	The theory and practice of strategic management for voluntary organisations, with nine case studies and an extensive bibliography.
J. M. Bryson (1995) *Strategic Planning for Public and Non-profit Organizations*. San Francisco: Jossey-Bass.	A US writer but many ideas are very relevant to the UK voluntary and community sector, with a focus on strengthening and sustaining performance.
KnowHow NonProfit website pages on strategy: www.knowhownonprofit.org/organisation/strategy	A great resource giving an overview of all of the critical aspects of developing a strategy.
The Public Leadership Inquiry (2010) Leading Agility: www.publicleadershipinquiry.co.uk	Research into strategic leadership competencies.
Copps J. and Vernon B. (2010) *The Little Blue Book: NPC's guide to analysing charities, for charities and funders*. London: New Philanthropy Capital. www.philanthropycapital.org/publications/improving_the_sector/charity_analysis/Little_blue_book.aspx?dm_i=59B,3I1A,KFH4X,AX3N,1	Two practical approaches to internal fitness assessment.
Venture Philanthropy Partners (2001) *Effective Capacity Building in Nonprofit Organizations*. Reston: Venture Philanthropy Partners. www.vppartners.org/learning/reports/capacity/assessment.pdf	
Ash F., Copeman C., Patel A. and Smith S. (2008) *Tools for Success: Doing the right things and doing them right*. London: Cass CCE. www.cass.city.ac.uk/research-and-faculty/centres/cass-centre-for-charity-effectiveness/tools-for-success	This toolkit and support package is intended for use by any small voluntary and community organisation wishing to invest in its long-term sustainability.
La Piana D. (2008) *The Nonprofit Strategy Revolution: Real-Time Strategic Planning in a Rapid-Response World*. Nashville: Fieldstone Alliance. www.lapiana.org/strategy/real-time-strategic-planning	A really interesting approach to keeping your strategy fresh and relevant.
Osterwalder A. and Pigneur Y. (2010) *Business Model Generation*. The Business Model Resources to help research the internal and external environment Canvas: www.businessmodelgeneration.com/canvas	A very different (one page) lens through which to look at your organisation and consider future strategic options.
Bell J., Masaoka J. and Zimmerman S. (2010) *Nonprofit Sustainability: Making strategic decisions for financial viability*. San Francisco: Jossey-Bass.	An interesting way of considering both mission impact and financial viability.

Marketing

Bruce I. (2011) *Charity Marketing: Delivering income, services and campaigns.* London: Institute of Chartered Secretaries and Administrators	Explains how using marketing principles to underpin every aspect of activity can transform how not-for-profit organisations meet need and achieve their objectives.
Eliot J. and Piper R. (2008) *True Colours: Uncovering the full value of your organisation.* London: NCVO.	A guide to help organisations appreciate the broader value of their organisation and communicate it to different audiences.

Funding and finance

Abdy M. and Mayall H. (2006) *Funding Better Performance.* London: NCVO.	Drawing on six case studies, this report gives practical guidance to both funders and voluntary and community organisations on the skills and approaches needed to ensure both parties get better results.
Palmer P. (2005) *The Good Financial Management Guide.* London: NCVO.	A user-friendly guide to managing financial resources and all the financial tools and techniques.
NCVO's Sustainable Funding Project website: www.ncvo-vol.org.uk/sfp	Introduces the themes of sustainable funding, related organisational development issues and information on planning, and contains relevant signposts to further sources of information.
Bruce I. (2010) *The Art of Raising Money.* London: NCVO.	Theories and techniques developed in the commercial world will help you to transform your fundraising and income generation so that it is sustainable, integrated and rewarding.

Evaluation, outcomes and performance measurement

Wainwright S. (2002) *Measuring Impact: A guide to resources.* London: NCVO.	A really clear guide to impact and its measurement, with a very useful 'resources' section.
Charities Evaluation Services (2008) *Practical Monitoring and Evaluation: A guide for voluntary organisations.* London: Charities Evaluation Services. www.ces-vol.org.uk/publications-research	A fairly high-level guide to monitoring and evaluation for voluntary and community organisations. It takes the form of an accessible 'how to' guide to monitoring and self-evaluation. The Charities Evaluation Services (CES) website also has a wide range of publications on measuring impact and making your strategy outcome focused.

Sanfilippo L. and Cooper M. (1st edition) Murray R. and Neitzert E. (update) (2009) *Tools for You: Approaches to proving and improving for charities, voluntary organisations and social enterprise.* London: New Economics Foundation. www.neweconomics.org/publications/tools-you	Provides an overview of a range of different approaches to quality and impact assessments.
Rickey B., Lumley T. and Ní Ógáin E. (2011) *Bright Spots in Impact Measurement: A journey to greater impact: Six charities that learned to measure better.* London: New Philanthropy Capital. www.philanthropycapital.org/publications/improving_the_sector/improving_charities/Journey_to_impact.aspx?dm_i=59B,MDD2,KFH4X,1T8IH,1	Case studies on effective impact measurement.
Niven P. (2010) *Balanced Scorecard: Step-by-Step for Government and Nonprofit Agencies.* Hoboken: John Wiley and Sons.	A clear explanation of how not-for-profit organisations can develop balanced scorecards to help them track the most important elements of their strategy.
Balanced scorecard case studies: Diana Memorial Fund: www.excitant.co.uk Case study on Motor Neurone Disease Society: www.ap-institute.com	An overview of how these two organisations developed their balanced scorecards.

Collaborative working

Linden R. M. (2002) *Working Across Boundaries: Making Collaboration Work in Government and Nonprofit Organizations.* San Francisco: Jossey-Bass.	A practical guide with a focus on getting relationships and processes right.
NCVO collaborative working web pages: www.ncvo-vol.org.uk/advice-support/collaborative-working	A range of introductory guides on collaboration: • partnership working • should you collaborate? • joint working agreements • staffing a collaborative project.
Chadwick M. (2012) *On Board the Merger Bus.* London: Cass CCE. www.cass.city.ac.uk/research-and-faculty/centres/cass-centre-for-charity-effectiveness/resources/thought-pieces	A thought piece explaining that while mergers are not for the faint-hearted, they should not necessarily be avoided.

Governance

NCVO (2010) *Good Governance: A Code for the Voluntary and Community Sector* (2nd edition). London NCVO.	The code sets out best practice in trusteeship and, while it is not mandatory, organisations that comply with the code are invited to state this in their annual reports.
Dalton D. (2011) *Good Governance: A practical guide for trustees, chairs and CEOs*. London: NCVO. Akpeki T. (2005) *Good Governance Action Plan Workbook*. London: NCVO.	Two practical guides to improving governance.
Blake G., Robinson D. and Smerdon M. (2007) *Living Values Training Pack*. London: NCVO.	A training pack and pocket guide for trustees on living their organisation's values.

Participation and user involvement

New Economics Foundation/UK Participation Network (1998) *Participation Works! 21 techniques of community participation for the 21st century*. London: New Economics Foundation. www.neweconomics.org/publications/participation-works	This handbook explores what participation really means, and what makes it really happen. It contains 21 proven techniques and includes how to choose between them, how to use them properly and where to go for more information.
NCVO participation web pages: www.ncvo-vol.org.uk/strategy-impact/learn/participation	Involving service users and other people in your work can generate new ideas, challenge your assumptions and help you to ensure that your products or services are as relevant as possible.

Performance management

Eliot J. and Pottinger J. (eds) (2008) *From Here to There: Managing change in third sector organisations*. London: NCVO.	A guide aimed at anyone involved in managing change. It contains introductions to different types of change to enable readers to choose the right approach and plan for a change that lasts.
Armstrong M. and Baron B. (2004) *Managing Performance: Performance Management in Action*. London: Chartered Institute of Personnel and Development.	An excellent general book on performance management, relevant to all sectors.

Resources

Resources to help research the internal and external environment

Griffith Gray M. and Williams N. (2007) *Future Focus series*. London: NCVO.	Future Focus is a series of introductory pocket guides to help organisations understand important trends that may impact on them in the future.
Copeman C. and Griffith Gray M. (2007) *Looking Out: How to make sense of your organisation's environment*. London: NCVO.	This practical guide helps voluntary sector leaders improve their knowledge and skills in understanding the changes going on around their organisation.
Copeman C. (2006) *Picture This: A guide to scenario planning for voluntary and community organisations*. London: NCVO.	A practical guide full of information, tips, templates and tools to help you plan and run scenario-planning workshops and build the learning into future strategies.
NCVO UK Civil Society Almanac: http://data.ncvo-vol.org.uk/	An annual overview that provides in-depth analysis and statistics on the latest civil society trends.
Megan Griffith Gray M. (2009) *Surviving in a Changing Environment. NCVO members' briefing 2009/10*. London: NCVO.	Reflections and approaches to developing a strategic response to a changing external environment.
Jochum V. and Wilding K. (2012) *The Road Ahead? A review of the voluntary sector's operating environment for NCVO members, 2012*. London: NCVO.	Developed using PEST analysis, this digital-only report identifies and explains seven key forces and trends that are shaping the sector. (NCVO members only – visit www.ncvo-vol.org.uk/membership for more details.)
NCVO Third Sector Foresight website: www.3s4.org.uk/drivers	A searchable bank of over 100 drivers affecting the voluntary and community sector.
DEMOS: www.demos.co.uk	Research and analysis on public services, identity, science and technology, arts and culture, global security, and cities and public space.
IPPR: www.ippr.org.uk	Research and analysis on social, political, economic, health, media, education and sustainability issues.
Institute for Social and Economic Research: www.iser.essex.ac.uk	Production and analysis of long-term trends and research on social change.
International Training and NGO Research Centre: www.intrac.org	Research, policy and analysis on new trends affecting civil society.
The Joseph Rowntree Foundation: www.jrf.org.uk	Research and analysis on social trends, including poverty, housing, social care, governance and public services.
KnowHow NonProfit: www.knowhownonprofit.org/organisation/strategy/externalanalysis	Tools and techniques to help understand and respond to the external environment.
National Council for Voluntary Organisations: www.ncvo-vol.org.uk	Useful for analysis of how government policy relating to the voluntary and community sector is changing and other issues affecting the sector.

Organisation for Economic Co-operation and Development: www.oecd.org	Publications and statistics covering a wide range of economic and social issues.
Office for National Statistics: www.statistics.gov.uk	Home of official statistics, reflecting Britain's economy, population and society at national and local level.
Policy Studies Institute: www.psi.org.uk	Research studies relevant to social, economic and industrial policy.
The Tomorrow Project: www.tomorrowproject.net	Research, analysis and communication on future trends, including globalisation, employment, sustainability, politics and government, media, technology and social exclusion.

All websites accessed October 2012.

Resources
Further support

Cass Centre for Charity Effectiveness

The Cass Centre for Charity Effectiveness at Cass Business School (Cass CCE) develops and disseminates knowledge and understanding of the voluntary, community and social enterprise sector through: academic research; postgraduate programmes; leadership development; consultancy.

Our research is primarily problem based and empirically oriented, and its findings are incorporated into the curriculum and developing consultancy solutions.

Cass CCE offers five postgraduate diploma/MSc programmes dedicated to charity effectiveness:

- Charity Accounting and Financial Management
- Grantmaking, Philanthropy and Social Investment
- Charity Marketing and Fundraising
- NGO Management
- Voluntary Sector Management.

The Cass CCE Consultancy and Talent Development team works with boards, organisations, teams, individuals and sector associations, helping them to create real change by transferring knowledge, experience and leading-edge thinking.

Our consultants specialise in: strategic thinking, collaborations and mergers; governance; leadership development; operational effectiveness.

We also offer short courses, master classes and events throughout the year to bring the latest thinking.

Please call Cass CCE on 020 7040 0901 or email casscce@city.ac.uk or visit www.cass.city.ac.uk/cce for more information.

Cass CCE: intellectual leadership, developing talent, enhancing performance.

KnowHow NonProfit

KnowHow NonProfit enables an online community of individuals and organisations to share knowledge, expertise and inspire best practice within the voluntary and community sector.

Whether you are a leading expert in your field, interested in building on your existing knowledge and skills, or just starting out, KnowHow NonProfit offers a new interactive pathway to individual, organisational and sector development.

Share your knowledge and expertise in online discussions or by adding case studies on the wiki platform, or take an online training course in StudyZone.

Find out more at www.knowhownonprofit.org

NCVO members get special access to the KnowHow NonProfit StudyZone.

NCVO consultancy

NCVO consultancy provides high quality support, facilitation services, workshops and training.

Their services and solutions have been developed for the voluntary sector, and they have years of experience in supporting infrastructure and front-line charities to deliver benefits for their beneficiaries.

NCVO principally offers support in the areas of:

- strategy and creating impact
- governance and trustee support
- impact measurement and reporting
- campaign effectiveness and influencing
- collaborations with the public and private sectors
- sustainable funding strategies
- new ways of working and generating income.

Find out more at www.ncvo-vol.org.uk/consultancy

NCVO members get a 20% discount on the consultancy service.

The Directory of Approved Consultants

NCVO's Directory of Approved Consultants lists individuals and organisations that have experience working with the voluntary sector. All featured consultants have passed NCVO's approval process.

Areas of expertise include strategic planning and project management.

Find out more at www.ncvo-vol.org.uk/dac

NCVO members receive a free copy of the print edition of the Directory of Approved Consultants.

NCVO newsletters

NCVO produces free email newsletters on a range of different topic areas, including leadership and strategy, employment and governance.

Register at www.ncvo-vol.org.uk/signup

NCVO members also receive fortnightly email bulletins on news and developments in the voluntary sector.

Find out more about NCVO membership at www.ncvo-vol.org.uk/ membership